FOR REFERENCE

Do Not Take From This Room

Key Words in Hinduism

Key Words in Hinduism

Ron Geaves

Georgetown University Press / Washington, D.C.

As of January 1, 2007, 13-digit ISBN numbers will replace the current
10-digit system.
Paperback: 978-1-58901-127-4

Georgetown University Press, Washington, D.C.

Library of Congress Cataloging-in-Publication Data

Geaves, Ron.
  Key words in Hinduism / Ron Geaves.
     p. cm.
  ISBN 1-58901-127-9 (alk. paper)
  1. Hinduism—Dictionaries. I. Title.
  BL1105.G43 2006
  294.503—dc22
                            2006006889

This book is printed on acid-free paper meeting the requirements of the
American National Standard for Permanence in Paper for Printed Library
Materials.

13 12 11 10 09 08 07 06   9 8 7 6 5 4 3 2
First printing

Printed in Great Britain

Contents

Preface **vii**
The Glossary **1**

PREFACE

During the course of teaching a number of religions in four higher education institutions, one common feature has been the number of students who have told me that they found the mastering of religious terminology in so many unknown languages and involving unfamiliar concepts to be the most daunting part of the module. In view of this, the *Key Words* series was created to provide a glossary of terms for five religions.

The religions have been chosen to reflect the main traditions that are studied both in school and at university in the English-speaking world. One glossary also contains the key specialist terminology used in the academic study of religion. It is hoped that the glossaries will prove to be useful and informative resources for anyone studying religion up to undergraduate level, but that they will also provide a fascinating pool of information for anyone interested in religious practice or belief, whether for the purpose of gaining qualifications or simply in the personal pursuit of knowledge. Each glossary therefore provides an exhaustive exploration of religious terminology in a way that is accessible but also provides an overall in-depth understanding of the religious tradition.

Although Hinduism is now provided with its own separate book, even so the glossary's completion is arbitrary, as each religion covered by the *Key Words* series is a conceptual framework for viewing the world that commands a vast vocabulary. This is particularly true of Hinduism, where the names of gods alone would create a book considerably larger than the present work. My choice of terms has been determined by school and undergraduate curricula, and the length of each definition has been dictated by the fact that this is a glossary and not a specialist religious dictionary. Inevitably, however, some concepts and persons involved more than a short passage in order to clarify their significance and highlight their importance within the world of their respective religion. Some terms reflect my own interests as a scholar, especially those that belong largely in the world of popular religion, more familiar in village vernaculars than in various forms of orthodoxies. I have also decided to transliterate the terms into the English alphabet without diacritics. Although this may irritate the specialist scholar, especially those whose work is textual study, it remains part of the spirit of the original *Continuum Glossary of Religious Terms*, which was to provide acceptable variant spellings to non-specialists.

Finally, I would like to thank Catherine Barnes, whose patience and support has been remarkable; Janet Joyce who provided the original opportunity for this project to grow from its inception to completion; and Continuum for providing the means for the glossaries to appear in their various editions.

A

Abhiseka   The rite of bathing the MURTI that is a central part of temple worship. Each day the *murti* will be woken, bathed in various sacred substances such as sesame oil or curd. It will then be adorned in new clothes, jewelry and a sacred thread. (*See also* PUJA)

Acarya / Acharya   *Lit. one who teaches by example*. Title given to a prominent or exemplary spiritual teacher or a religious scholar who teaches correct conduct based on observance of DHARMA. Traditionally it was necessary to be able to expound the UPANISHADS, the BRAHMASUTRAS and the BHAGAVAD GITA in order to receive the title of *acarya*. One of the four orders of renunciates established by Shankara.

Adivasis   The numerous tribes of indigenous people whose culture can be traced back over half a million years. Their practices and beliefs have influenced popular Hinduism and may reflect the original religion of the Indian subcontinent.

Advaita Vedanta   The non-dualistic system of VEDANTA taught by SHANKARA based on his monistic interpretation of the famous pronouncement of the *Chandogya Upanishad:* TAT TVAM ASI (that thou art). Shankara argued that this referred to complete identity of BRAHMAN, ATMAN and the world. Any form of perception that does not perceive the reality of this monistic unity is under the sway of MAYA or illusion.

Agama The collection of scriptures acknowledged as the sacred canon of the SHAIVITE tradition and believed to have been uttered by SHIVA or PARVATI himself or herself. They provide the authority for most of the rituals and doctrines of specific Shaivite and Tantric sects. (*See also* TANTRA)

Aghori A SHAIVITE sect of SADHUS that live at cremation grounds, drink and eat from a human skull and offer polluting substances such as blood, meat, alcohol and sexual fluids to the deities they propitiate. The intention is to obtain powers through practising taboos. This type of asceticism has virtually died out in India but is maintained by the Aghoris in VARANASI.

Agni The Vedic god of fire who mediates between gods and humans. He is the principal god invoked in the sacrifice along with SOMA. Agni is the ultimate priest who brings men and gods together by consuming the sacrifice offered by BRAHMINS.

Ahamkara / Ahankara The sense of ego or 'I-ness'. The awareness of individual being that can be transcended by the experience of the self's true identity. (*See also* YOGA)

Ahimsa Non-violence, harmlessness or respect for the sanctity of life. In Hinduism it has been popularized by the stance of GANDHI in his campaign of SATYAGRAHA (holding on to the truth) against the British raj. *Ahimsa* had long been one of the early and necessary stages of the discipline of YOGA and had developed to be the central doctrine of Jainism.

Akharas Orders of Shaivite warrior ascetics that developed from the ninth century to the eighteenth in response to the Muslim invasions of India. They were six in number and are called Ananda, Niranjani, Juna, Avahan, Atal and Nirvani. (*See also* SADHUS)

Alvars The twelve Tamil VAISHNAVITE poet-saints who lived between the seventh and tenth centuries travelling from temple to temple singing the praise of VISHNU.

Amrit   *Lit. nectar of immortality*. Originally churned by the gods and demons from the cosmic ocean of milk at the beginning of the world, *Amrit* is believed to be present in the human body at the *talu-chakra* (the uvula) and can be drunk by *yogis* through a special technique. This is particularly associated with NATH YOGIS. (*See also* CHAKRA; YOGI)

Ananda   *Lit. bliss*. One of the three qualities of BRAHMAN in VEDANTA philosophy. The other two are SAT and CHIT. These three qualities give rise to the name of SATCHITANANDA to describe the ultimate reality.

Anasakti   The doctrine of selfless action. Gandhi believed that it was the central message of the BHAGAVAD GITA. (*See also* KARMA)

Anrta   The Vedic concept of chaos believed to pre-exist RTA or cosmic order. *Rta* also indicates social order and when this breaks down there is a return to social and cosmic chaos. (*See also* DHARMA)

Antaryamin   According to RAMANUJA, the inner controller, or the soul within the soul which is the form of VISHNU manifested in the world in the heart of all beings. (*See also* VISHISHTADVAITA)

Anviksiki   The intellectual analysis of Vedic knowledge utilizing logic that is taught within the six orthodox schools of philosophy. (*See also* ASTIKA; DARSHAN)

Apasmara   The dwarf that represents ignorance and is danced upon by SHIVA in the form of NATARAJA, the Lord of the Dance.

Apaurusya   The belief that the VEDAS do not have human authorship but are a timeless revelation that contains all human and divine knowledge. It is this belief that marks the *Vedas* out as SHRUTI and leads many contemporary Hindus to describe them as a revelation of God. However, this idea may have developed after the influence of Islam.

Apsaras   In Hindu cosmology, the universe is inhabited by various kinds of beings that inhabit various realms. It is possible for souls to be reborn into any of these worlds depending upon KARMA. The *apsaras* are heavenly nymphs.

Apurva   Similar to the theory of KARMA, *apurva* is believed to be the sacred power that creates the result of successfully performing the Brahminic sacrifice. *Apurva* will eventually lead to the reward of heaven after death but it cannot bring MOKSHA or liberation from SAMSARA. The theory of *apurva* is particularly associated with the MIMANSA school of Philosophy. (*See also* BRAHMIN; ASTIKA)

Aranyakas   *Lit. belonging to the forest.* The SHRUTI texts attached to the BRAHMANAS (1000–600 BCE) which were composed by sages in the forests. They move away from the ritual dimension of the VEDAS to a more speculative introversion in order to seek answers to the meaning of existence. They form part of the Vedic canon and provide the ideas developed by the UPANISHADS.

Arjuna   The third of the five PANDAVAS brothers who were the sons of King Pandu. Their struggle to reclaim their kingdom forms the central plot of the Hindu epic, the MAHABHARATA. Arjuna's dialogue with KRISHNA provides the setting and the subject matter for the BHAGAVAD GITA.

Artha   Worldly or material success usually associated with wealth. Although shunned by the renunciate, *artha* is a legitimate goal of the householder along with DHARMA (duty), KAMA (sexual pleasure) and MOKSHA (liberation). Some Hindus consider all four to be the gift of God bestowed upon the righteous person.

Arti   A ceremony in which lighted ghee lamps and incense are swung on a tray in offering to the deity or a guru whilst singing verses of praise. *Arti* forms a vital constituent of both temple and home worship. (*See also* PUJA)

Arya Samaj   A Hindu reform movement founded by Swami DAYANANDA in 1875. The movement is opposed to folk Hinduism based on the teachings of the PURANAS and attempts to restore Hinduism as taught in the VEDAS. The movement was important in counteracting the criticisms of Hinduism made by Christian missionaries and has influenced the revival of Hindu nationalism prevalent in India today. The organization has founded schools and Vedic training institutions, and has generally involved itself in political and cultural activities with the aim to promote Vedic culture. (*See also* BRAHMO SAMAJ)

Aryan   Sometimes used to indicate those who know the spiritual values of life, but usually refers to the Aryan people believed to have invaded North India and conquered the DRAVIDIAN settlements that already extended from Sind to Bihar. The term derived from *Arya* (noble) used by the authors of the VEDAS.

Asana   Various postures that are considered beneficial when practising meditation. The science of HATHA YOGA has developed a system of complex postures which when combined with breathing exercises are believed to lead to liberation.

Ashram   *Lit. shelter.* A retreat place or hermitage used for spiritual development and often the centre of teaching for a particular GURU or sect.

Ashrama   The four ideal stages of life consisting of BRAHMACHARYA, GRIHASTHA, VANAPRASTHA and SANNYASIN. The first stage is that of student and celibate in which higher caste Hindus would have traditionally studied under a religious preceptor; the second stage is householder life; the third stage begins when the children have married and the parents begin to move towards renunciation, giving up their worldly activities and devoting more time to religious activities; the final stage is that of complete renunciation. Very few contemporary Hindus follow the ideal. The emphasis is on householder life although many older married couples may follow some kind of *vanaprastha*. (*See also* VARNASHRAMDHARMA)

Astika   The Hindu orthodox who accept the Vedic revelation. They usually belong to one of the six orthodox schools of Hindu philosophy. *Astika* excludes Buddhists, Jains and Sikhs. (*See also* NASTIKA)

Asuras   A term originally used to describe the supreme gods but which is now applied to the demons and anti-gods of the Vedic hymns who were the enemies of the ARYAN gods. According to the BRAHMANAS both the DEVAS and the *asuras* were created by PRAJAPATI, the creator god. The *asuras* made offerings to themselves and the *devas* made offerings to each other. This developed into a divine hierarchy in which the *devas* accepted offerings and provided reciprocal rewards whereas the *asuras* were essentially selfish.

Atharva Veda   The fourth of the VEDAS, recognized as SHRUTI at a later date, which is famous for magical incantations and spells. Many of these may have been passed on from pre-ARYAN religious traditions, as there is little emphasis on the sacrificial rite that dominates the other three *Vedas*.

Atman   The soul, the real self, or the principle of life. In the UPANISHADS, *atman* is used as distinct from BRAHMAN when it refers to the eternal or ultimate power within the individual rather than in the cosmos. The *Upanishads* posit the unique metaphysical idea that *atman* and Brahman are one entity. The difference is only in perspective. *Atman* is microcosmic whereas Brahman is macrocosmic.

Aum   The supreme MANTRA, also known as *pranava*, the seed *mantra*, and said to contain all the sounds of other *mantras* within it. It is made up of three sounds: 'A', 'U' and 'M' that represent all spoken speech or the root of all creation. Thus OM or AUM is the essence of all creation or the immanent Divine, and is, therefore, the Supreme Being in the form of speech. OM is also the seed *mantra* or primeval *mantra* as it does not associate the devotee who repeats it with any particular deity. It is therefore regarded as the *mantra* or sound of BRAHMAN, the Absolute Being. OM is at the beginning and end of all Hindu recitations of Sanskrit scripture and is printed at the front and back of all religious books. It is also engraved on the walls and doors of religious buildings. (*See also* SABDA BRAHMAN)

Avatar   *Lit. a descent.* The VAISHNAVITE tradition of Hinduism is shaped by its belief in the incarnation of VISHNU into ten forms. However, other traditions suggest that incarnations of Vishnu are countless. The most famous are the human incarnations, RAMA and KRISHNA. However, popular Hinduism also acknowledges that SHIVA and the Goddess have taken various human forms. The belief in avatars predisposes Hindu disciples to regard their respective GURUS as incarnations of the Divine.

Avidya   The condition of ignorance or having no vision that is the situation of those not liberated from the cycle of rebirth. In ADVAITA VEDANTA it arises from the influence of MAYA and is destroyed by the knowledge that BRAHMAN and ATMAN are identical.

Ayodhya   A city in Northern India believed to be the birthplace of RAMA and therefore one of the important TIRTHAS or pilgrimage sites for Hindus. In recent years Ayodhya has been the centre of activity for Hindu communalism and anti-Muslim feeling gathered around the issue of the Babri mosque that was built on the site of an older Hindu temple.

Ayurveda   Medical science derived from the Vedic teachings. *Ayurveda* is essentially a system of medicine derived from herbs. However, the science of *ayurveda* is concerned with everything to do with health, including longevity and fertility. It also includes complex purification practices.

B

Baiga   A village priest who serves a local deity or GRAM DEVATA. A *baiga* does not have to belong to the BRAHMIN caste nor is his religious activity associated with sacrifice or propitiation of the high gods. Most of his religious work will be involved with exorcism of evil spirits, curses and perceived supernatural causes of disease, infertility and misfortune. (*See also* BHUT)

Benares   *see* VARANASI.

Bhabhut   The ashes from a fire offering. *Bhabhut* can be used in a variety of ways. It is sometimes placed on the forehead but some ascetics cover their complete bodies in fire ash. In some popular traditions, *bhabhut* is used as a means to remove possession by evil or malevolent forces. (*See also* BHUT; HAVAN; VIBHUTI)

Bhagavad Gita   *Lit. The Song of the Lord*. The most famous and popular of all Hindu scriptures, it consists of a dialogue between KRISHNA and the warrior ARJUNA. It is the eighteenth chapter of the epic the MAHABHARATA, and was probably written somewhere in the first millenium BCE. It is regarded so highly that many Hindus consider it to be an UPANISHAD or part of the SHRUTI canon. The *Bhagavad Gita's* authorship is attributed to the sage VYASA. The narrative develops around a dialogue in which Krishna reveals himself as the AVATAR to his friend Arjuna in the middle of a battlefield. The dialogue begins in response to Arjuna's dilemma as he faces the possibility of a battle in which he will fight against friends, relatives and teachers. Krishna quickly takes the discussion past the immediate crisis to a syncretistic exposition of the ways to discover the absolute. The *Bhagavad Gita* is particularly important to BHAKTI movements as Krishna finally indicates the superiority of the devotional path over and above all others.

Bhagvan / Bhagwan / Bhagavan   Generally speaking, *Bhagvan* is used as distinct from the impersonal BRAHMAN and is the most common appellation for the personal God or ISHWARA. *Bhagvan* is the term used by Hindu theists to describe a supreme being who creates, maintains and destroys the cosmos but who also intervenes in human life to save devotees by the power of grace. The most common forms of *Bhagvan* are the various manifestations of VISHNU and SHIVA.

Bhajan   A devotional song often used in communal temple worship. Many of them were written by the poet-saints of the mediaeval BHAKTI / SANT tradition and describe their intense experience of close intimate relationship with God as either a formless reality or an AVATAR. The most common *bhajans* are those of the female mystic, MIRABHAI. (*See also* NIRGUNA; SAGUNA)

Bhakta   A devotee or one who practices devotion (BHAKTI). Devotion may be given to the personal God or ISHWARA, both with and without form. Most *bhaktas* fall into the two categories of VAISHNAVITE or Shaivite, that is devotees of the various forms of VISHNU and SHIVA. However, there are countless manifestations of goddess worship. (*See also* SHAIVISM)

Bhakti   The path of devotion or love or the attitude of loving adoration towards the divine. Most forms of *bhakti* posit the possibility of close proximity or even union with the divine through ecstatic love and service. *Bhakti* may be expressed towards an ISHWARA or a human GURU often believed to be a manifestation of the divine. Devotion is praised by KRISHNA in the BHAGAVAD GITA and many Hindus consider it to be the easiest and most enjoyable way to worship God. *Bhakti* has entered the popular expression of Hinduism and can be regarded in its multifarious forms as the most prevalent form of the religion.

Although it reached out to the people through the popular saint cults of the mediaeval period that criticized the Brahminical grip on access to the divine, the thread of *bhakti* can be picked up in the earlier classical periods of Hindu history. (*See also* BHAKTI YOGA; RAMAYANA; SANT; SHIVA; VISHNU)

Bhaktivedanta Prabhupada Swami   (1896–1977). The founder of the ISKCON (International Society for Krishna Consciousness) movement, popularly known as HARE KRISHNA in the West. Prabhupada represented a fifteenth-century tradition of ecstatic KRISHNA worship known as GAUDIYA VAISHNAVISM, founded in Bengal by CAITANYA. Caitanya himself is regarded as an AVATAR of Krishna and RADHA in one body. In 1965, Prabhupada travelled to North America to fulfil the instructions of his guru to spread Krishna consciousness throughout the world. Since then the ISKCON movement has successfully established itself throughout the world and has become arguably the most successful form of Hinduism outside India. Although originally a movement followed only by hippies in North America and Western Europe, it is now successfully integrated into the diaspora Hindu communities that have been created by migration. Prabhupada is also a successful commentator on the BHAGAVAD GITA and SRIMAD BHAGAVATUM.

Bhakti Yoga   The path to loving devotion. The way to achieve pure love of God. The BHAGAVAD GITA expounds the doctrine that there are various routes to discover God. These are primarily the three YOGAS. Bhakti yoga is clearly indicated by KRISHNA as the easiest and most enjoyable path that is available to all human beings including outcastes and women. This provided a revolutionary inspiration against the hegemony of the Brahmins and their belief that only the twice-born castes could achieve liberation through renunciation. *Bhakti yoga* introduces the idea of loving service to a personal Lord who bestows his grace on human beings and allows the possibility of a close bond of love between the human and the divine. (*See also* BHAKTI; JNANA YOGA; KARMA YOGA; MARGA; SANT)

Bharat Mata   *Lit. Mother India.* Hindus generally refer to India as *Bharat*, or the holy land. In this respect, Hinduism is a geographical religion in which the divine is manifested in countless ways on *Bharat*'s sacred space. The whole of India is a complicated network of local and national shrines that present the full complexity of Hinduism. The concept of *Bharat Mata* was picked up by the Hindu nationalist movements in their successful attempt to create a common Indian identity and remove the British from India. ʹ

Bhedabhedavada   The doctrine of identity in difference expounded by RAMANUJA in opposition to SHANKARA's monistic idea of complete identity of ATMAN and BRAHMAN. Ramanuja perceived Brahman to be both the same and different from *atman*. The individual self (*jiva*) is distinct from Brahman but cannot exist without God as the inner controller and essence of being (*atman*). There is therefore inseparability but not identity between God and the self. (*See also* ADVAITA VEDANTA)

Bheru   The ferocious aspect of SHIVA usually represented as a stone painted with lead oxide which often resembles the Shiva LINGAM. This form of Shiva traditionally functions as the guardian of wells and is more commonly found in rural Hinduism.

Bhima   One of the PANDAVAS, or sons of King Pandu, who were robbed of their kingdom by their cousins, the Kauravas. The conflict between the two groups is recorded in the MAHABHARATA. Bhima is the second eldest of the brothers but his character is marked by gluttony and violence. (*See also* ARJUNA)

Bhishma   The common grandfather to both the PANDAVAS and the Kauravas in the epic MAHABHARATA. Bhishma aligned himself for reasons of DHARMA with the Kauravas in the battle of Kurukshetra and he contributed to ARJUNA's unease in regard to the righteousness of fighting for his rights. At the end of the battle, YUDHISHTHIRA, the eldest Pandava, asks KRISHNA to teach him the path of *dharma*. Krishna declines and instructs Yudhishthira to seek advice from Bhishma on his death bed.

Bhopa   *See* BAIGA.

Bhut Supernatural beings or the ghosts of human beings that are envious of the living and haunt them. Many of the religious practices of popular rural Hinduism are concerned with protection or exorcism of these beings. (*See also* BAIGA)

Brahma The first part of the TRIMURTI. The creator god or the creative aspect of BRAHMAN. He is depicted as having four heads and four arms. In each arm he holds a drinking vessel, a bow, a sceptre and a book. His VAHANA is a swan. In the PURANAS, he is described as the source of all scriptures but it is generally believed in popular mythology that he appears from the lotus that emerges from VISHNU's heart at the birth of creation. Brahma then manifests the universe. At the end of the universe, Brahma withdraws back into the lotus and Vishnu enters a deep sleep. The cycle is known as the day and night of Brahman. In spite of Brahma's high status as the creator-god, he has never been as popular as Vishnu or SHIVA and there are only two temples to the deity in India.

Brahma Sutras A collection of aphorisms attributed to the sage Badarayana concerning BRAHMAN, which along with the UPANISHADS forms the basis of VEDANTA philosophy. MADHVA, RAMANUJA and SHANKARA all wrote commentaries on the *Brahma Sutras* that develop their various schools of Vedanta.

Brahmabhuta *Lit. to become Brahman.* This is the goal of Hindu religious aspirations. It is in this state that the being attains complete liberation from SAMSARA and its consequent suffering. The essence of the message of the UPANISHADS is to become BRAHMAN, or more accurately to realize that one always was and is Brahman. (*See also* ATMAN; MOKSHA)

Brahmacharin / Brahmacarin A celibate student in the first stage of life who maintains chastity, sexual abstinence or a life of spiritual discipline whilst studying with a teacher. Any person who maintains celibacy for religious reasons. (*See also* ASHRAMA; BRAHMACHARYA)

Brahmacharya / Brahmacariya The first of the four stages of life or ASHRAMAS in which a 'twice-born' boy lives as a celibate student under the guidance of a teacher in order to study the VEDAS. According to tradition he can remain there for a period of nine to thirty-six years. *Brahmacharya* is also used to describe anyone who maintains the state of celibacy in order to sublimate their sexual energy for religious purposes.

Brahman The power present in the whole universe or the ultimate reality behind the creation. Brahman is indescribable but has the three qualities of SAT, CHIT and ANA. There is nothing beyond Brahman who is the ultimate being that both transcends and pervades the universe. Enlightened sages or YOGI discover their oneness with that supreme being by purifying individual consciousness so that it can flow back into the universal ocean of pure awareness that is Brahman. This state is MOKSHA or eternal freedom from the phenomenal world. In this state the endless round of rebirth comes to an end. (*See also* ATMAN; SAMSARA; VEDANTA)

Brahmanas One of the four sets of scriptures in the SHRUTI category that form the VEDAS. These scriptures interpret the sacred formulas of the *Vedas* and provide the precise rules and regulations for performance of ritual. They also contain the original myths that were developed in later centuries.

Brahmin The highest class or VARNA from which the priests are drawn. They are the custodians of both the sacred text of the VEDAS and the rituals believed to be essential for the correct ordering of society. The authority of the BRAHMINS is originally described in the oldest Hindu creation myth described in the RIG VEDA. In this myth human beings are created from the cosmic sacrifice of the *purusha*. The brahmin caste is said to have sprung forth from *purusha*'s head.

Brahmo Samaj A nineteenth-century reform Hindu sect founded by Ram Mohan Roy in 1827. Roy attempted to establish a Hinduism based on ethical and moral teachings that moved away from the popular polytheistic Hinduism of the masses. Roy was strictly monotheistic and claimed that true Hinduism was incorporated in the UPANISHADS. His movement had little mass appeal but found support amongst the newly emerging merchant middle classes. The Brahmo Samaj can be seen as a reaction to European colonial domination and an early attempt to establish a Hindu national identity. (*See also* ARYA SAMAJ)

Brhadaranyaka Upanishad   *Lit. the great forest.* One of the earliest UPANISHADS, written between 600–300 BCE, in which the idea that all the gods are manifestations of one supreme being is proclaimed for the first time.

Buddha   Although the Buddha criticized aspects of the Brahminical tradition, asserting that the only true BRAHMIN is a person of outstanding spiritual and moral character rather than someone born into a particular VARNA, he has been incorporated into the Hindu pantheon of deities. Buddha is regarded in Hinduism as the ninth incarnation or AVATAR of VISHNU.

Buddhavatara   *Lit. the age of the Buddha.* BRAHMIN priests in India begin their daily oblations with the prayer 'in this age of the Buddha I offer my oblation', in spite of Buddha's powerful critique of their practices. (*See also* BUDDHA)

Buddhi   The first manifestation of PRAKRITI. *Buddhi* is the intellect or 'higher mind'. It is from the *Buddhi* that the ego or AHAMKARA arises, from there emerge the mind (MANAS), the five senses of perception, the five organs of action and the five gross elements that form creation. This hierarchical cosmology was first fully developed in the SAMKHYA school of philosophy but now pervades most Hindu metaphysics in some form. It is given universality by the BHAGAVAD GITA, which describes KRISHNA's nature as consisting of the same categories.

C

Caitanya Mahaprabhu / Chaitanya Mahaprabhu A Bengali VAISHNAVITE reformer (1486–1533 CE) whose ecstatic devotion was focused on KRISHNA. He followed the philosophy of a thirteenth-century Bengali Vaishnavite named Nimbarka. This doctrine posited that God was both the same as, but different from, individual souls. Caitanya preached devotion to Krishna expressed through ecstatic singing of KIRTAN. He is believed by many Hindus to be an incarnation of Krishna. ISKCON devotees believe him to be the combined incarnation of Krishna and RADHA and their historical founder. (*See also* BHAKTIVEDANTA SWAMI; VAISHNAVISM)

Caste *See* JATI.

Caturvarna *Lit. four classes*. The name for the orthodox Hindu social system that divides humanity into four classes or VARNAS, namely BRAHMIN, KSHATRIYA, VAISHYAS and SUDRA.

Chakra The belief prevalent in YOGA philosophy that the body contains a subtle body with centres or wheels of energy connected by three central channels of lifeforce (PRANA). There are believed to be six or seven *chakras* located at the perineum, genitals, solar plexus, the heart, the throat, between the eyes and at the top of the head. Some yoga techniques attempt to raise the KUNDALINI (serpent power) up the central channel to the thousand-petalled lotus at the crown of the head. It is here that, so it is believed, the bliss of liberation is experienced by the practitioner.

15

Chakravartin   *Lit. one who is at the centre of the wheel.* The ruler of the universe or universal monarch. Kingship has played an important role in ancient Hindu DHARMA. The king was believed to play an intermediary role between his subjects and the divine. The qualities of deities were often given to kings and many kings were also AVATARS such as KRISHNA and RAMA. A king aspired to be the ruler of the universe or chakravartin. Buddha's birth was heralded by the prophesy that he would either be a chakravartin or a world-renouncer.

Chanda   *See* VEDANGAS.

Chandas   A branch of Vedic literature that explains the complicated metre of the Vedic verses. These explanatory texts were developed to allow young BRAHMINS to study. (*See also* JYOTISA; KALPA)

Chandogya Upanishad   One of the oldest UPANISHADS that deals in detail with the nature of the relationship between BRAHMAN and ATMAN. It is an important text for the VEDANTA schools that have argued over the meaning of its pronouncement 'TAT TVAM ASI' ('that thou art').

Chela   A village exorcist. One who is skilled in the art of overcoming the effects of sorcery through the use of MANTRAS.

Chinmoyananda, Swami   One of the Hindu teachers that came to the West in the 1960s. He was a disciple of the VEDANTA teacher, Sivananda of Rishikesh, who became popular amongst the young truth-seekers from the USA and Europe who visited India to study YOGA in the early 1960s. Shri Chinmoy, as he is often called, began centres throughout the world and attracted publicity when the rock band, Santana, became his followers.

Chit / Cit   *Lit. consciousness.* The second of the three qualities of BRAHMAN and ATMAN as in SATCHITANANDA (Truth, consciousness and bliss). Truth is unalloyed consciousness existing in its own pure state rather than having become identified with the world and the body through the vehicle of the senses. The idea that the supreme being is best expressed as *Satchitananda* is expounded fully by SHANKARA.

Curail   A female ghost that often possesses young women in pregnancy. It is believed that the *curail* is either a woman who has died in childbirth or died without children. She is envious of women that are bearing children. These kinds of village beliefs are dealt with by special practitioners who are proficient in exorcism.

D

Dakshina The fee paid to a BRAHMIN or other religious officiate for performing a religious ceremony. It can also be a financial offering to a temple or a GURU.

Dakshineshwara The name of the nineteenth-century temple complex dedicated to KALI built four miles outside Calcutta. In 1852, a young BRAHMIN was appointed assistant priest and went on to become one of Hinduism's most important influences in the twentieth century. Renamed RAMAKRISHNA on initiation by a wandering *Advaitin* monk, he is considered by many Hindus to be a contemporary AVATAR. Consequently Dakshineshwara is now an important pilgrimage centre. (*See also* VIVEKANANDA)

Dalits The self-chosen name for the members of the 'scheduled castes' or 'untouchables'. *Dalit* means oppressed, and in recent times this group have managed to organize themselves into a powerful political force resisting the economic and social injustice they have suffered because of their position in the Hindu caste system. (*See also* HARIJANS)

Dan Body or physical resources. Usually used in association with MANAS and *tan* (mind and wealth) to indicate the commitment considered essential on the path of BHAKTI. Surrender to the will of the deity in order to be the recipient of grace is fundamental to the *bhakti* path. This is practically possible through the commitment of a proportion of one's physical, mental and material resources to the path of devotion.

Danda *Lit. a stick.* *Danda* can refer to the fear that is in all beings placed there by divine order to ensure that they do not wander away from the ideals of DHARMA. It is also used for the stick or staff carried by wandering holy men, particularly those of the Shaivite tradition. There may be a connotation here that the stick can be used to reprimand a religious recalcitrant and bring them back to the way of *dharma.* (*See also* SHAIVISM)

Darshan *Darshan* is a vital part of the Hindu religious experience and forms the raison d'etre of pilgrimage and temple worship. *Darshan* means the vision of the deity and it is believed that when the worshippers or devotees come before the MURTI or a GURU, they are blessed with a vision of the divine. Rituals are carried out at the installation of a *murti* in order to invite the presence of God to inhabit the deity. Thus the *murti* is brought to life and becomes the form of the god that it represents. When Hindus visit the temple they enter the presence of the divine, so *darshan* carries the connotation of not only seeing the divine, but also being seen by the divine.

Darshan Shantras The six systems of orthodox Hindu philosophy. By the medieval period the various intellectual traditions that had developed from a range of commentaries on Vedic and Sutric literature had been codified into six schools of orthodoxy. These are not rigid systems and there will be many opinions within one school; indeed, the ideas of the various schools are interwoven into the blanket of everyday Hinduism. (*See also* ASTIKA; MIMANSA; NASTIKA; NYAYA; SAMKHYA; VAISESHIKA; VEDANTA; YOGA)

Dasanamis Ten orders of Shaivite ascetics believed to have been founded by SHANKARA in the ninth century. They are known for their scholarship and pursuit of the absolute. (*See also* SHAIVISM)

Dasaratha The legendary king of AYODHYA and the father of RAMA. The king died of heartbreak after being tricked by the jealousy of his second wife, KAIKEYI, who made him promise to banish Rama from the kingdom in favour of her son, Bharat. These incidents trigger the saga of Rama described in the RAMAYANA.

Dassera / Dassehra / Vijay Dashmi   The ten-day festival associated with the victory of RAMA over RAVANA. However, most Gujarati Hindus celebrate it as the festival of DURGA, also called Amba in Gujarat, known as NAVARATRI (nine nights). At the end of this period the festival of DURGA PUJA takes place alongside the celebration of Rama's victory. It is held in September–October.

Dayananda, Swami   1824–83. The founder of the Hindu reform movement, ARYA SAMAJ. After running away from home in order to avoid an arranged marriage, he met with a GURU who advised him to commit himself to the correct interpretation of the VEDAS. He went on to become a considerable Sanskrit scholar. In 1875 he founded the Arya Samaj in Bombay. He attacked the corruptions that he perceived existing in nineteenth-century Hinduism but unlike other Hindu reform movements such as the BRAHMO SAMAJ, he was not influenced by Christianity. He preached a message of return to the religion of the *Vedas* based upon his own interpretation.

Deva   A god or deity; usually one of the major gods of the Hindu pantheon. Hindus will choose from the pantheon of gods the one that they feel most drawn to worship. However, this does not negate worship of other deities on special occasions. There may be a tradition of worship towards a particular god within a family or caste group, but it is important to remember that most Hindus believe the gods to be aspects of one supreme being so worship of one deity does not exclude the worship of others. (*See also* DEVI)

Devata   A minor divinity or demi-god usually associated with a DEVA. They are not malevolent and are usually described in the minor texts of mythology. Particular *devatas* may be worshipped regionally or within particular sub-castes. (*See also* GRAM DEVATAS)

Devi   A female deity usually of the higher pantheon. Most of the male deities have a female partner such as LAKSHMI or PARVATI. However, KALI and DURGA are goddesses in their own right and have a considerable following amongst Hindus. (*See also* DEVA)

Dharamsala A religious hospice or guest-house used to accommodate travellers and pilgrims. Also the name of a town in the Himalayas famous as the home-in-exile of the Dalai Lama and the Tibetan community that has accompanied him.

Dharana Used in a similar way to Buddhist terminology to describe one-pointed concentration on a single object, often a MANTRA or an ISHVARA. The term is most commonly used by the YOGA school.

Dharma A cosmic principle variously translated as righteousness, right conduct, duty, and way of life or religion. The source of *dharmic* obligations is the VEDAS which subscribe certain ritual actions to the BRAHMINS to maintain both social and cosmic order. The reward for the performance of these rituals is heaven but *dharma* is carried out for its own sake and failure to do so results in sin (PAP). However, *dharma* is usually regarded as context and caste specific. Most Hindus would consider themselves bound to perform *dharmic* actions that are required according to their status in society. For those that belong to BHAKTI or other religious movements, *dharma* is usually associated with religious activity that will bring liberation closer. The association with religion has become the common definition of *dharma* and many Indians will use the term in the context of a particular religious identity and practice such as Sikh *dharma*, Jain *dharma*, etc. *Dharma* is often associated with caste or VARNA as it has also come to mean correct ritual, social or ethical action associated with a particular subgroup. (*See also* JATI; KARMA; PUNYA; VARNASHRAMDHARMA)

Dharma Sastras A branch of SMRTI literature written around 300–600 CE that deals with the precise code of behaviour for high-caste house-holders. They are also a source for jurisprudence and have been used by assemblies of BRAHMINS to determine Hindu law and legislation. They contain the important LAWS OF MANU (*Manu Smrti*).

Dhyana A common term used to describe the vast variety of medita-tional practices available within Hinduism. Generally the term is used to describe practices that lead to SAMADHI or union with the eternal life-principle.

Diksha   An initiation ceremony usually associated with becoming a SANNYASIN or renunciate. It is also used to describe any initiation where a devotee is accepted by a GURU. Various sects founded by a guru and maintained by a lineage will also usually have an initiation ceremony on entry. (*See also* SAMPRADAYA)

Divali / Diwali   One of the major Hindu festivals which come at the end of the year, around October, and lasting for five days. It is known as the Festival of Lights as lamps are ceremoniously lit and presents exchanged. Traditionally there are often large firework displays. The festival celebrates particular events in the life of VISHNU and one day is given to worship of his consort, LAKSHMI, the Goddess of wealth. The last day is usually celebrated as sisters' day.

Dravidian   The ancient culture of South India that is believed to predate the ARYAN invasion. Many aspects of DRAVIDIAN culture have survived and South Indian Hinduism contains many features not present in the North.

Durga   A principal manifestation of the Goddess depicted as riding on a tiger and carrying many weapons. In spite of being a war goddess and associated with killing demons, Durga assumes a feminine and benign aspect in popular iconography. The more fierce aspect of the Goddess is KALI. Both are associated as forms of the consort of SHIVA known as PARVATI. However, although goddess worship is closely aligned with Shaivism, Durga is worshipped in her own right and has become one of the major deities of contemporary Hinduism, particularly in Bengal. (*See also* SHAIVISM; SHAKTI)

Durga Puja   The festival in honour of DURGA that takes place within the larger festival of DASSERA held in August–September to mark the end of the monsoon. The ninth day of Dassera is traditionally used to worship Durga. The festival is popularly celebrated in Bengal where there is a strong tradition of Durga worship.

Dvaita   A theistic form of VEDANTA taught by MADHVA (1238–1317). Madhva's doctrine of dualism posits that the selves and the universe are both distinct from BRAHMAN. Each self is also different from Brahman and remains individual even when liberated. It is even possible that some selves may never be liberated. This is a unique perspective in Hindu doctrine. In other respects Madhva's doctrines are similar to RAMANUJA.

Dvapara / Dwapara   Hinduism deals with vast expanses of time based on the day and night of BRAHMA. According to the PURANAS, each Day of Brahma consists of one thousand manvantaras. Each manvantara is further divided into four YUGAS or ages of decreasing righteousness. Dvapara is the third age and lasts for 864,000 years. All of these ages are cyclical and thus the cosmos has no beginning or end in Hindu cosmology.

Dvarka / Dwarka   A famous pilgrimage site on the north-west coast of India associated with KRISHNA. It is one of the seven most sacred sites of pilgrimage. Dvarka is believed to be Krishna's capital. Recent excavations have found a large city, now submerged in the Arabian Sea, that dates back to c.1600 BCE. (*See also* TIRTHA)

Dvija   *Lit. 'twice-born'*. The term is applied to the three highest VARNAS (BRAHMINS, KSHATRIYAS and VAISHYAS) who are allowed to study the VEDAS and receive the sacred thread at puberty.

E

Ekasringa   An early animal form or avatar of VISHNU who manifested as a unicorn to save the first man, MANU, from the great flood which destroyed the rest of humankind.

G

Ganapati *See* GANESH.

Gandharva Veda A sacred text that deals with the art of music and dance. Although known as a VEDA, it is, in fact, an UPAVEDA; texts that deal with lesser knowledge rather than the higher transcendent knowledge of the *Vedas*.

Gandhava Semi-divine musicians who occupy one of the heavenly realms. In Hindu cosmology there are countless different worlds that are populated by heavenly and demonic beings. However, all these realms are impermanent and the occupants will eventually die and be reborn elsewhere. (*See also* SAMSARA)

Gandhi A Hindu reformer (1869–1948) who stressed the doctrine of AHIMSA (non-violence) and inspired the movement to free India from British rule. He was born in the state of Gujarat and went to London where he studied Law. Whilst in Britain, he was influenced by the spiritual teachings of the BHAGAVAD GITA and the Sermon on the Mount. After his studies he departed for South Africa where he lived for twenty-one years. He was deeply shocked by his experience of Apartheid and began to develop his ideas to free people from political oppression whilst maintaining a deep commitment to non-violence. On return to India, he inspired Indians to free themselves from British rule through the application of passive resistance based on the principle of *ahimsa*. His political and religious philosophy became known as SATYAGRAHA. Gandhi's tolerant attitude towards all of India's religious communities resulted in his assassination in 1948 by a militant nationalist Hindu.

Ganesh / Ganupati / Ganapati   The god of wisdom, prudence and salvation whose name is derived from *Ga* meaning 'knowledge' and *Na* meaning 'salvation'. He is one of the most widely worshipped deities in Hinduism and easily recognizable by his elephant head. Ganesh is depicted as a short, large-bellied man with an elephant head that has only one tusk. He is usually seated cross-legged and his skin is yellow. His four arms contain a conch shell, a discus, a club and a lotus flower. He is usually shown with a small bowl of the Indian sweet known as the *ladoo* to represent prosperity. He is also accompanied by a rat which is his vehicle (VAHANA), to symbolize the union of the large with the small. He is regarded as the deity who removes obstacles, therefore he is often placed in a position where he is the first deity to be seen in a temple and worshippers can use his DARSHAN to pray that the god will remove the obstacles from devotees so that they can approach the other deities. Hindu rituals usually begin with an invocation to Ganesh and many Hindus begin their daily activities by a short prayer that invokes the god's name. According to the PURANAS, Ganesh is the younger son of SHIVA and PARVATI, but he is not mentioned in Hindu scriptures before 500 CE and only become popular in the later mediaeval period. The *Shiva Purana* recounts the legend of his elephant's head by explaining that when Shiva was away for thousands of years practicing austerities, Parvati appointed her son to guard her door whilst bathing. On the return of Shiva to his family, Ganesh, who did not know his father, refused him entry to the house. The irate father cut off his son's head, and when confronted with his error by the inconsolable Parvati, restored his son to life with the head of a young elephant.

Ganga   The Indian name for the Ganges, the most sacred of India's rivers. Commonly known as Ganga Mai, or Mother Ganga, the river is believed to be a goddess whose descent to earth was controlled by flowing through SHIVA's matted locks. Many towns on the Ganga are sacred sites and some of them are amongst Hinduism's most famous pilgrimage places. The most famous is VARANASI. Millions of pilgrims bathe in the Ganga and may perform the SHRADDHA ceremony on its banks (annual homage to a departed ancestor). Most Hindus will want to drink Ganga water immediately before dying. (*See also* HARDWAR)

Gangotri   The source of the Ganga in the Himalayas and a famous pilgrimage site. (*See also* GANGA)

Garbha-griha   *Lit. womb-house.* The innermost sanctum of a Hindu temple where the MURTI or image of the god is installed. This structure will usually be located at the back of the temple. In traditional temple design the shrine room is topped by a tapering ornate tower that can be seen from the outside of the temple. (*See also* MANDIR; SHIKHARA)

Garuda   The king of the birds and the mount of VISHNU. Garuda is usually depicted as an eagle.

Gaudapada   The guru of SHANKARA's guru whom Shankara describes as his supreme guru. Gaudapada's teachings seem to be influenced by Buddhism even though Shankara himself vehemently opposed Buddhist doctrine. (*See also* ADVAITA VEDANTA)

Gaudiya Vaishnavism   This form of VAISHNAVISM developed in early mediaeval Bengal and expressed the ideal of ecstatic devotion to KRISHNA. The ideal of devotional love is expressed in the relationship between RADHA and Krishna. The devotee longs for Krishna with the emotional intensity of Radha for her absent Lord. The greatest exponent of this tradition was CAITANYA (1486–1533) who is often regarded as an AVATAR of Krishna and Radha in one being. The goal of liberation is attained by the Gaudiya followers in this world by maintaining an ecstatic experience of divine love. This is often expressed through ecstatic singing and dancing. The Gaudiya tradition is best known in the West through the activities of ISKCON or the HARE KRISHNA movement.

Gayatri Mantra   A famous Sanskrit mantra from the RIG VEDA used in daily worship by many Hindus. It is also ritually repeated by a twice-born male youth at the sacred thread ceremony. The MANTRA is as follows: *Om Bhur Bhuvah Swahah Om Tat Savitur Varenyam Bhargo Devasya Dhimahi Dhiyo Yo Naha Prachodayat* (We concentrate our minds upon the most radiant light of the supreme god, who sustains the earth, the interspace and the heavens. May this god activate our thoughts). Traditionally the *mantra* is recited in praise of the sun-god, but most contemporary Hindus would refer it to the supreme being, BRAHMAN.

Ghat   A flight of steps leading down to a river usually associated with assisting pilgrims to bathe. A daily bath is a prescribed ritual for Hindus. Many will take their ritual bath in a river. Some *ghats* are used for cremation. The most famous are in VARANASI. (*See also* TIRTHA)

Ghee / Ghi   Clarified butter considered to be propitious as it is a product of the cow and used by Hindus for cooking and sacrificial purposes. The oil is used to make the small candles that are placed on a tray and swung in veneration of the gods. Ghee is also used for cremation. (*See also* ARTI)

Gita Govinda   A famous poem about the love of KRISHNA and RADHA composed by Jayadeva, a court poet who wrote under the patronage of the Bengali king, Lakshmanasena (1179–1209). Its themes are union, separation and the longing for reunion. It is therefore regarded as symbolic of the love of the devotee for the Lord. (*See also* BHAKTI; GOPIS)

Gopis   The childhood playmates of KRISHNA at the time that he lived in exile in Gokula, identified as Vrindavan by CAITANYA. Ancient stories depict the amorous adventures of Krishna with the cowherd girls. In later VAISHNAVITE traditions (from the twelfth century onwards) the love between the *gopis* and Krishna becomes the symbol of the all-embracing love of the devotee for the supreme Lord – the ultimate goal of BHAKTI. This passionate play of love reciprocated by the Lord himself is encapsulated in the love that existed between Krishna and his favourite *gopi*, RADHA. (*See also* GAUDIYA VAISHNAVISM; VAISHNAVISM)

Gorakhnath   A famous mediaeval Shaivite YOGI who taught in North-West India and is the reputed founder of several ascetic movements usually defined as Nath or KANPHATA. Gorakhnath has been deified in popular tradition and is considered to be a miraculous offspring of SHIVA. There are countless legends of his birth and the miracles that he performed in his lifetime. He is considered to be the founder of the HATHA YOGA system and is also held in high regard by Tibetan Buddhists. His guru was Matsyendranath and there are countless stories depicting the relationship of guru and disciple. The Naths became famous for their supposed mastery of psychic and miraculous powers achieved through their austerity and practice of yoga, and were later criticized by Guru Nanak, the founder of Sikhism, on the grounds that such practices promoted ego rather than humble surrender to the will of God. (*See also* NATH YOGI; SHAIVISM)

Goswamis   The six close disciples of CAITANYA (1486–1533 CE), the ecstatic Bengali devotee of KRISHNA. The Goswamis developed the theology of intense devotional love as manifested through the erotic tales of Krishna and RADHA. They travelled to VRINDAVAN with Caitanya and helped develop that city as one of the great centres of Krishna devotion. There are temples in Vrindavan associated with all six goswamis and many of the SAMPRADAYAS (sectarian traditions) in the city claim that they originated from one of them.

Gotra   Exogamous group within a caste or JATI. It is the *gotra* membership that controls marriage partners. Generally in rural India it will extend over several neighbouring villages.

Gram devata   A village deity or godling whose powers are confined to the locality. The *gram devatas* are worshipped in order to remove everyday afflictions of village life. In thousands of Indian villages, these lesser manifestations of the divine are worshipped everyday by Hindus who consider the great gods of Hinduism too remote or unconcerned with their daily affairs. Many of the *gram devatas* are female. (*See also* BHUT; MATA; OHJA)

Grihastha / Gristhi / Grhastha   A *grihasthi* is a householder, the second and most emphasized of the four stages of life that ideally should be followed by a Hindu. After completing the student period, which was traditionally passed under the tutelage of a Brahmin GURU, the male Hindu should marry, live as a householder and raise a family. There are religious commitments expected in this stage of life. An ideal householder should restrain the senses, practice non-violence, and maintain equanimity and detachment. The difference between a householder and a renunciate is one of scale. The householder should aspire to the renunciate's ideal. However, the householder has ritual obligations whereas the renunciate has none. (*See also* VARNASHRAMDHARMA)

Gun   A quality or attribute which arrives as a gift from God rather than being an innate quality of the personality. Such spiritual or virtuous attributes are believed to arrive by the grace of God to those who follow the path of intense devotion. (*See also* BHAKTI)

Guna   One of three forces or qualities that make up all of inner or outer nature. Everything which is created is an interplay of these three *gunas*: SATTVA (harmony); RAJAS (activity); TAMAS (inertia). They intermix in infinite varieties to create the quality of a being or entity. Hindu philosophy has developed classifications defined according to these three qualities. For example, food can be *sattvic*, such as fresh vegetables, fruit or products of the cow; these will promote spiritual development. On the other hand, it can be *rajasic* (meat) which promotes energy, activity, anger or lust; whilst *tamasic* food (decayed) will promote sloth or inertia. Many of these classifications are based on KRISHNA's discourse to ARJUNA in the BHAGAVAD GITA, although the theory of the *gunas* is older and was used in SAMKHYA philosophy.

Guru   *Lit. darkness to light.* A teacher or preceptor. Someone who becomes one's spiritual instructor. The disciple/teacher relationship lies at the heart of traditional Hindu culture. There are many different kinds of guru: one could have a music guru, for example. However, it is in the realm of religion that the term is most popularly used. A guru could be a family priest or one who teaches the rituals of Hindu tradition, but, in Hinduism the guru is often associated with the divine. In the Shaivite tradition, it is believed that the guru is the physical form of SHIVA sent to save souls from the cycle of birth and rebirth. Similarly, the role of the guru is considered essential in VAISHNAVISM. Some later developments in Vaishnavism claimed that the guru was more important than God, as it was the guru who held the key to salvation. The true guru should be able to impart spiritual knowledge; be completely free from selfish motives, and considerate of the spiritual welfare of all other human beings. Many such gurus have taught paths to God or self-realization that have created countless sects or SAMPRADAYAS. Although many Hindu gurus have functioned within the caste system, there have been famous examples that have challenged its supremacy in Hindu society and attracted disciples from all sectors. Contemporary gurus are often claimed to be divine by their followers, but they tend to be universal in that they often allow anyone to become a follower regardless of caste, gender or nationality. Many have traveled to the West to extend the range of their teachings. (*See also* DIKSHA; SATGURU; SHAIVISM)

Gurukulu   Traditional forest universities believed to have been maintained by sages in ancient Vedic culture. The idea of the *gurukula* was re-established in the late nineteenth century by the conservative wing of the ARYA SAMAJ, a Hindu reform movement. The schools were established to promote Hindu unity and ARYAN culture. Children entered as young as eight years old and remained for a sixteen year training in Sanskrit and Vedic culture. The period of training was meant to coincide with the traditional BRAHMACHARYA phase of VARNASHRAMDHARMA. (*See also* SWAMI DAYANANDA)

Gyana   Spiritual knowledge. Sometimes it is understood that such knowledge can be learned by the study of scriptures but it is also used to describe knowledge that arises from direct experience of God (BRAHMAN) or realization of the Self (ATMAN). The relationship between these two informs different theories concerning spiritual knowledge. (*See also* JNANA; VEDANTA)

Hansa   A mythological swan that can separate milk and water. The swan is used as a symbol for the soul that is able to discriminate the real from the unreal. *Hansa* is therefore sometimes a title for an enlightened GURU who possesses the same quality of discrimination. (*See also* VIVEKA)

Hanuman   The monkey warrior-chief and son of the Wind-god, VAYU, who faithfully served RAMA and SITA as recounted in the great epic, the RAMAYANA. Although possessing supernatural strength and other extraordinary powers, it is for his personal devotion and service to the AVATAR, Rama, that Hanuman is best loved. In the BHAKTI tradition, he is regarded as the personification of devotion. In TULSIDAS's Hindi version of the *Ramayana*, Rama offers Hanuman the traditional Hindu life-goals of wealth, pleasure, DHARMA and spiritual liberation as rewards of his service. Hanuman refuses them all and asks for devotion. In Hindu temples that contain the MURTIS of Rama and Sita, he is usually present as a kneeling monkey with hands folded in adoration at their feet. Very often he is placed at the door to Hindu temples as the guardian deity but there are also specific Hanuman temples. He is also the patron deity of wrestlers. (*See also* RAMACHARITAMANASA)

Harappa   One of the two principal cities of the old Indus Valley civilization excavated in the 1920s. The Harappa civilization is believed to have reached its peak somewhere around 2500–2000 BCE and disappeared within a thousand years. The Indus valley civilization was vast and covered nearly one million square miles of territory, including most of Northern India and Pakistan and extending down into Gujarat. Although little is known about their religion, there is some speculation, arising from excavated figurines and seals, that the people may have worshipped a variety of goddesses and a proto-SHIVA figure who sits in a yogic-type posture. (*See also* ARYAN; DRAVIDIAN)

Hardwar / Haridwar   A famous pan-Indian pilgrimage town that is one of the seven sacred sites revered by all Hindus. Hardwar is built on the banks of the Ganga in the Himalayan foothills and situated in the state of Uttar Pradesh. Hardwar is one of the sites for the KUMBHA MELA, the four-yearly Hindu festival in which millions gather to bathe in the Ganga and co-exist for several days with gatherings of SADHUS and holy men and women from all over India.

Hare Krishna   The popular name for the ISKCON movement derived from the first two words of the MANTRA that is chanted by the devotees and believed to contain the real name of God that can save devotees in the KALI YUGA (age of darkness). The mantra is *Hare Krishna, Hare Krishna, Krishna, Krishna, Hare, Hare. Hare Rama, Hare Rama, Rama, Rama, Hare, Hare.*

Hari   An affectionate name used by the devotees of VISHNU to describe the personal Lord, especially his human AVATARS, RAMA and KRISHNA. (*See also* VAISHNAVISM)

Hari-Hara   The fusing of VISHNU and SHIVA into one composite being containing the form and qualities of both.

Harijans   *Lit. sons of Hari.* Gandhi used this term to describe untouchables, as he perceived them to be the blessed of God. Discrimination on the grounds of untouchability is outlawed by the Indian Constitution, but remains prevalent especially in rural India. Untouchables have organized themselves effectively into social and political movements but they prefer to call themselves DALITS.

Hariva-msa A scripture that supplements the great epic, the MAHAB-HARATA. It recounts tales of KRISHNA's early life, whereas the *Mahabharata* is only concerned with his involvement in the politics of the great battle when he is already king of DVARKA.

Hatha Yoga Although best known in the West as a system of physical postures used in some yogic disciplines, and practised for reasons of health, in fact, Hatha Yoga was the system of postures and breathing exercises developed by the NATH YOGIS, a well-known Shaivite renunciate order, as a specific path to spiritual liberation. (*See also* GORAKHNATH; SHAIVISM)

Havan The sacrificial ceremony in which ghee and grains are offered into fire. Performed by a BRAHMIN priest it is the main ritual associated with many life cycle rituals and Hindu ceremonies. (*See also* YAJNA)

Havan Kund The container in which the HAVAN fire is burned.

Hiranya Kasipu The wicked demon and tyrannical father of PRAHLAD, the child-devotee of VISHNU. Hiranya Kasipu is destroyed by NARASIMHA, the half-man, half-lion incarnation of Vishnu. Hiranya Kasipu had practised intense austerities to be granted the wish of virtual immortality. He could not be killed by a human or an animal, in the daytime or in the night. Thus Vishnu had to manifest a unique AVATAR to destroy him and save the persecuted Prahlad. This event is celebrated in the Hindu festival of HOLI.

Hitopadesh A collection of moral tales often involving animals, similar to Aesop's fables.

Holi The Hindu festival of colours, celebrated in Phalguna (March–February). Traditionally everyone will throw coloured powder dyes over each other. There are also bonfires and street processions. The festival is associated with disorder and anarchy. In some parts of India normal authority relations are overturned for the day and wives will be seen beating their husbands in the street. Religiously the festival is associated with the manifestation of NARASIMHA, the man-lion AVATAR of VISHNU, to protect his devotee, PRAHLAD, from his demon king father. (*See also* HIRANYA KASIPU)

Homa / Hom   *See* HAVAN.

I

Indra The sky and storm god of the early Vedic period and the most important of the old Vedic gods, though he later declined in importance. However, by the time of the RIG VEDA he had become the great warrior-god of the ARYAN civilization. He is closely associated with SOMA, the unknown drug of Vedic ritual. Indra is the ideal of the fighting hero, the KSHATRIYA, and a king by his might of conquest. Although king of the gods in the Rig Veda period, he has now declined in importance to being the god of rain. Indra's position in the Hindu pantheon has been supplanted by VISHNU.

Isha Upanishad One of the collections of UPANISHADS, famous for its statement that the whole world is pervaded by BRAHMAN. The *Isa Upanishad* was a great favourite of Mahatma GANDHI who claimed that he based his life on its first verse: 'All this whatsoever moves on earth, is pervaded by the Lord. When you have renounced this, then you may enjoy. Do not covet the wealth of anyone'.

Ishvara / Ishwara Usually translated as the Lord or master, *ishwara* refers to the various personal forms of God worshipped by a devotee in the BHAKTI tradition as opposed to the impersonal BRAHMAN. SHANKARA, the founder of ADVAITA VEDANTA, considered the *ishwara* to be a manifestation of the cosmic impersonal Brahman who creates, sustains and destroys the universe. It is this god that is worshipped by the devotee through ritual action, but at the end of creation *ishwara* returns into the formless Brahman. This emanationist theory of *ishwara* is denied by RAMANUJA, the great proponent of VAISHNAVISM, who claims that *ishwara* and Brahman are one and the same being. In some VAISHNAVITE traditions, the form of the personal *ishwara* is the ultimate being. The formless God exists as an emanation of the ultimate form. This position reverses that of Shankara. (*See also* VEDANTA)

ISKCON The International Society for Krishna Consciousness founded by BHAKTIVEDANTA Swami in the late 1960s. Although first perceived as a bizarre hippy cult, the HARE KRISHNA movement, as it is more popularly known, has now achieved world-wide respectability in the Hindu community. In Britain, the centre of the movement is Bhaktivedanta Manor, donated by George Harrison of the Beatles. The movement, although remaining predominantly white converts, has its roots in GAUDIYA VAISHNAVISM, a mediaeval KRISHNA BHAKTI movement established in Bengal. The most famous proponent and claimed founder of the movement is CAITANYA MAHAPRABHU. Today ISKCON is a respected part of Hindu tradition and supported by thousands of Hindu migrants who respect the way of life of the devotees and their strict adherence to Vedic ritual ceremonies. Although ISKCON devotees remain a presence on the streets of British cities singing KIRTAN and selling their publications, they are now accepted as part of contemporary Western culture and rarely attract the attention of the anti-cult movements or the media. Today the ISKCON movement is a prolific publisher and highly involved in educational activities to promote Hinduism.

Ista devata The personal god picked by the individual from the Hindu pantheon as his or her chosen deity. Individual worship will be offered to this deity daily, and the devout Hindu householder will repeat the name of this deity each morning before uttering any other word. (*See also* ISHVARA; MURTI)

Itihasa Purana The two great epics, the MAHABHARATA and the RAMAYANA are collectively known as *Itihasa Purana*. It can be argued that these two SMRITI texts have had far more influence on popular Hinduism than the Vedic texts.

J

Jagannath / Jagganath / Jaganatha   A form of KRISHNA worshipped in the famous temple in Puri, Orissa. Every year Jagannath is paraded in a huge processional carriage around the town. The MURTI is accompanied by elephants, holy men and horses as it is taken through the streets. Although a regional festival it has become famous throughout the whole of India.

Jagat   The cosmos of moving beings or creatures engaged in action. It is usually used to refer to the world of human beings but actually refers to the wider universe incorporated in the concept of SAMSARA.

Jamuna   *See* YAMUNA.

Janak   The famous king of Videha. He is named as the father of SITA in the RAMAYANA. He also appears in the BRHADARANYAKA UPANISHAD as an enlightened monarch who questions the sage YAJNAVALKYA concerning the reality of BRAHMAN. In Indian popular religious stories he often represents perfect detachment from the world although living in the midst of it.

Janeu   The sacred thread that goes over one shoulder and across the chest. It is invested at the UPANAYANA ceremony in which young males of the three highest VARNAS, believed to be twice-born, are initiated into adulthood and Hindu society. Recently some female activists have begun to initiate girls, claiming that this was the practice in early Vedic culture.

Janmashtami The festival that celebrates the birthday of KRISHNA.

Japa The repetition of the name of God or a MANTRA (sacred formula) as a means to spiritual experience or as a devotional exercise. It can also be done in silence as a meditation technique.

Jati *Lit. birth.* The complex hierarchical structure of Hindu society based on caste. Whereas Vedic society categorizes everybody into four VARNAS, the caste system further sub-divides the Hindu population into countless *jatis* based on occupational purity and impurity. Although the system is based upon occupation, it is hereditary and maintained by endogamy and commensality. It is believed that the Hindu's caste status is actually a property of the body itself and received through KARMA and rebirth. Every Indian village will maintain several castes living in close proximity but separate. They will range from the BRAHMIN at the top through to the untouchables at the bottom.

Jatra Annual fairs or festivals to village deities. People will come to make offerings and mark their foreheads with the holy ash kept near the shrine. The occasion is a holiday with events taking place such as wrestling competitions, magicians, fortune-tellers and plays of well-known folk stories.

Jijnasa The constant attempt to seek for spiritual knowledge (JNANA). *Jijnasa* is best expressed as the search for illumination or direct apprehension of ultimate reality.

Jiva mukti The state of having attained liberation whilst still alive. There is debate amongst various Hindu SAMPRADAYAS (sects) concerning whether this is actually possible, what is achieved, and how it differs from liberation after death. Most later mediaeval BHAKTI and SANT traditions emphasized the attainment of *jiva mukti*.

Jivatman The individual self or soul that separates from the body at death but continues to exist through endless rebirths until liberation or union with BRAHMAN is achieved. *Jivatman* differs from ATMAN in that it contains elements of individual personality carried over by KARMA into rebirth. (*See also* MOKSHA)

Jnana Generally used to describe knowledge or wisdom that comes from direct insight or experience of the divine or ultimate reality. However, the search for reality has developed into several sophisticated philosophies concerning the relationship between ATMAN, BRAHMAN and the world. *Jnana* is often used to describe the intellectual knowledge and understanding that arises from studying such systems. (*See also* JNANA YOGA)

Jnana Yoga One of the three major ways to salvation mentioned by KRISHNA in the BHAGAVAD GITA. It concerns developing methods to achieve the intuitive knowledge of the Absolute BRAHMAN as the ultimate reality. However, Hindus describe anyone who pursues a path to the knowledge of reality through intellectual disciplines and philosophical discourse, rather than the practices of BHAKTI (devotion), as a practitioner of *Jnana Yoga*. (*See also* BHAKTI YOGA; JNANA; KARMA YOGA)

Jnanadeva A thirteenth-century Maharashtrian BHAKTI poet inspired by his own personal experience of God. He wrote in Marathi and composed over one thousand devotional songs. He also wrote commentaries on the BHAGAVAD GITA and the UPANISHADS.

Jyotisa Vedic explanatory literature that introduces the BRAHMIN student to astronomical calculations needed to determine the correct time for rituals. (*See also* VEDAS)

Kabir (1398–1448) A NIRGUNA BHAKTI SANT famous for his uncompromising poems which preach the message that without direct experience of God within, all the externals of religion are pointless. He was extremely critical of the outer forms of religion but was equally revered by Hindus and Muslims for his uncompromising attacks on hypocrisy, caste, idolatry and empty rituals. 541 of his poems are included in the *Guru Granth Sahib*, the scripture of the Sikhs. Some Hindus believe that he influenced Guru Nanak, the historical founder of Sikhism and others have even suggested that he was Nanak's GURU. However, this is unlikely as Nanak was not born until 1469. Kabir was born in Benares to a weaver family that had converted to Islam. Tradition insists that he was a disciple of RAMANANDA, a VAISHNAVITE BRAHMIN teacher in direct lineage from RAMANUJA. Kabir, however, promoted the teaching that God is imminent in all beings including those of low caste. The sect that has developed from the teachings of Kabir is called the KABIRPANTHIS and their most famous temple is dedicated to the saint, situated in the heart of VARANASI. (*See also* VAISHNAVISM)

Kabirpanthis The Hindu sect that developed from the teachings of KABIR, the mediaeval SANT master of NIRGUNA BHAKTI. The Kabirpanthi is the Hindu sect which aspires to follow his teachings by not worshipping any Hindu deity or observing any rites or rituals common to Hindus, although in all other respects it conforms to a Vaishnava sect. (*See also* VAISHNAVISM)

Kaikeyi The mother of RAMA's elder half-brother, Bharat. Kaikeyi was jealous of Rama and used her seductive wiles on her husband, the king of AYODHYA, named DASARATHA. She wanted her son to rule the kingdom. The king succumbed and agreed to exile Rama into the jungle but Bharat refused to rule his brother's kingdom. These events set the scene for the stories that appear in the great epic, the RAMAYANA.

Kali The best-known form of the malevolent or dark aspect of the Goddess (SHAKTI), usually depicted as a young naked woman garbed only in a garland and short skirt both made up of skulls and bloody severed heads. Her hair is long and wild and her tongue protrudes red and bloody from her mouth. She is four-armed: two arms carry a sword and a severed head; the other two generally show her hands in MUDRAS (positions) of blessing. Kali, however, is not considered to be terrifying to her devotees in spite of her appearance. She dances upon the prone form of her consort, SHIVA, and thus represents the relationship of *Shakti* and Shiva or PRAKRITI and PURUSHA. *Shakti* dances the eternal manifestations of creation upon the supine motionless absolute. She therefore represents the endless motion containing and barely controlling chaos, disorder, death, decay and disruption. Her votaries seek protection from these aspects of existence. As in the Shaivite tradition, there is a Tantric form of Kali worship whose followers seek to subvert the usual Hindu categories of pollution and purity by seeking salvation through copulation and the consumption of meat and alcohol. The tradition of Kali worship is known throughout India but is strong in the state of Bengal. (*See also* KUNDALINI; SHAIVISM; TANTRA)

Kali Yuga The fourth of the four ages that comprise a cycle of time. The Kali Yuga is 432,000 years in duration and is associated with darkness and ignorance. It is believed that we are in the Kali Yuga at the present time and it will finally end with the coming of the tenth AVATAR of VISHNU named KALKI. However, TULSIDAS believed that the Kali yuga has the benefit of being the age when salvation is most easily achieved through the remembrance of the Name of God. (*See also* KALPA)

Kalika Purana   One of the PURANAS that deals with legends of the Goddess and practices of her worship. It tries to make a cohesive system of all the various forms of the Goddess worshipped in Hinduism by differentiating them as parts of the body of the one Goddess. There are also descriptions of how to perform human sacrifice. This is not a part of contemporary Hindu goddess worship but occasionally stories do emerge of isolated incidents. (*See also* KALI; SHAKTI)

Kalki   The tenth AVATAR of VISHNU who will appear at the end of the present KALI YUGA and re-establish an age of righteousness. It is believed that he will appear on a white horse.

Kalpa   Hindu belief has a cyclic view of creation and time. The universe passes endlessly through alternate periods of activity and repose, each one known as a *kalpa*, 8,649 million years in duration. Each period of activity and repose is known as a day and night of BRAHMA.

Kama   The Hindu god of sensual love. Originally he had a form but lost it after tempting SHIVA out of a long period of meditation. The gods had approached Kama to end the great ascetic's SAMADHI so that he would fulfil destiny and marry PARVATI, his eternal consort. Kama succeeded in tempting Shiva but was blasted by a ray of pure energy from the third eye of the angry god. Kama (sensual satisfaction) is also one of the four aims of life that can be fulfilled within householder life as long as it is regulated by DHARMA. (*See also* ARTHA)

Kama Sutra   A well-known manual of sexual conduct, seduction and positions for lovemaking that needs to read in the context of overall Hindu society. KAMA or pleasure is one of the legitimate aims of Hindu householder life as long as it is practised within the rules of DHARMA. Indulging in sex for its own sake is, however, usually considered to be an obstacle to the spiritual path.

Kanphata   A term used to describe the renunciate followers of GORAKHNATH. These yogis of the Shaivite tradition are also known as Gorakhnathi and Darsani but are more commonly called Nath in the

Punjab and the Himalayan region. Kanphata literally means 'split-eared' and refers to their practice of splitting the cartilege of their ears in order to wear the huge ear-rings that are one of their unique features. (See also HATHA YOGA; NATH YOGI; SHAIVISM)

Kapila   A sixth-century BCE sage reputed to be the founder of the SAMKHYA school of philosophy. Kapila is difficult to establish historically as he is semi-legendary and believed to be incarnation of VISHNU in some Hindu traditions. In the MAHABHARATA he is described as the son of BRAHMA, the Creator-god.

Karma   Derived from the Sanskrit root 'Kr' (to act or create), it refers to the immutable law of cause and effect which controls rebirth. *Karma* generally refers to all human activity and its consequences. It is a cosmic law that governs SAMSARA and ensures that all good and bad deeds bring their precise result. It is *karma* that governs rebirth. The accumulated *karma* of past actions has ensured the life that all living beings currently hold and the actions performed in this life ensure the next rebirth. Generally rebirth is seen in terms of caste. A better rebirth would be into a higher caste but it is possible to be reborn in non-human animal form as a consequence of actions performed in previous lives. It is also possible to be reborn as a god (DEVA) in a supernatural paradise. Hindus believe there are 8,400,000 species of life that the soul can be reborn into as a result of *karma*. (*See also* DHARMA; MUKTI)

Karma Marga   One of the three great paths to liberation along with BHAKTI and JNANA. *Karma marga* is the path to salvation through action. It is sometimes known as *Karma yoga*. The BHAGAVAD GITA teaches that it is achieved through selfless action, or not being attached to the fruit of action. However, in the MIMANSA school of philosophy it is associated with correct performance of Brahminic ritual. (*See also* NISHKARM KARMA)

Karma Yoga   *See* KARMA MARGA.

Kartikeya   One of the two sons of SHIVA and his consort, PARVATI. The other son is the elephant-headed god known as GANESH. Kartikeya is depicted with six heads and riding upon a peacock. He is often identified with the old Vedic war-god, SKANDA and is known in South India as Subramaniyam or MURUGAN.

Katha   A reading of scripture by a BRAHMIN priest that is sponsored by an individual Hindu or a family. It can take place either in the home or in a temple. The sponsor will pay the priest to carry out the reading either to fulfil a vow or to bring blessings to an occasion such as marriage or a new business venture.

Katha Upanishad   One of the principal UPANISHADS that contains the famous dialogue between the young BRAHMIN NATCHIKETAS and Death on the means to escape death and rebirth. This *Upanishad* also introduces the doctrine of grace as a prerequisite for salvation and thus introduces one of the most important elements of BHAKTI, the Hindu devotional tradition.

Khota   The displeasure of a village deity or GRAM DEVATA which can bring misfortune to the recipient. Continuous misfortune is often perceived to be the displeasure of a local deity. In such circumstances a specialist exorcist might be called in for assistance. (*See also* OJHA)

Kirtan   Congregational devotional singing that has become the popular medium of Hindu temple worship. It is likely that *kirtan* was introduced into popular Hinduism through mediaeval devotional movements who used it as a means to achieve ecstatic union with the divine and to promote their teachings. Today it is widespread as a part of Hindu practice. Most visitors to a Hindu temple in the West would observe *kirtan* taking place wherever Hindus gather for congregational worship. (*See also* BHAKTI)

Krishna   The eighth AVATAR of VISHNU who is considered by many VAISHNAVITES to be the fullest manifestation of the deity. Krishna means 'dark' or 'black' and he is worshipped in a variety of forms throughout India. Famous deities such as JAGANNATH and Behari are perceived as forms of Krishna, and the cities of PURI and VRINDAVAN are associated with their worship. Many of the cities that play a part in the Krishna legend are famous pilgrimage places. The legend states that Krishna was the son of VASUDEVA and Devaki but also the nephew of the tyrannical ruler, Kamsa. It had been prophesized that Kamsa would be slain by a nephew so the king ordered them all to be slain at birth. Krishna and his brother were saved through being adopted by the cowherd Nanda, and Krishna's subsequent amorous adventures with the cowherd girls are famous symbols of divine love. These stories are perceived as the LILA (play) of the manifest Lord and have been the centre of the teachings of several Vaishnavite sects. Krishna is eventually restored to his kingdom after slaying Kamsa. During this period he becomes involved in the feud between the PANDAVAS and the Kauravas that culminates in the battle of KURUKSHETRA. These events are told in the great epic, the MAHABHARATA. Other main sources for the life of Krishna are found in the PURANA, especially the SRIMAD BHAGAVATUM. One of the chapters of the *Mahabharata* is the famous BHAGAVAD GITA, in which Krishna expounds his teachings on liberation to ARJUNA, one of the Pandava princes. In the *Bhagavad Gita* Krishna is identified with the supreme being. Along with RAMA, he is the most popular deity worshipped by British Hindus and he has become well-known throughout the Western world through the preaching activities of the ISKCON movement. (*See also* GAUDIYA VAISHNAVISM)

Krishnamurti   A famous writer and lecturer on spirituality who has consistently refused to be acknowledged as a GURU. However, his books are a significant contribution to the extension of Hindu spiritual ideas to the West. Krishnamurti was brought up by the founder of Theosophy, Annie Besant, to be the AVATAR of the twentieth century. However, he refused to take part in the event organized by the Theosophists to announce him to the world. He is completely independent and has contributed to the development of a universal world spirituality.

Krodha   The vice of anger that along with LOBHA (greed) and MOHA (delusion) is considered to be at the heart of human failure to achieve progress on the path to liberation.

Krta yuga   One of the four ages, also known as SAT YUGA. This is the only one of the cycles of Hindu time where DHARMA is not corrupted to any degree. No disease exists and individual human lifespan lasts for four hundred years. (*See also* KALI YUGA; KALPAS; TRETA YUGA; YUGA)

Kshatriya The second of the four VARNAS after the BRAHMINS; they are the warrior class whose duty is to rule and to protect righteousness (DHARMA). The duty of the warrior was to protect the citizens through physical prowess and courage. The ultimate *kshatriya* would be the just and enlightened king, who in the Vedic period was often perceived as a deity. The duties of the just king are laid out in the epic scriptures, particularly the RAMAYANA and the MAHABHARATA. Many such kings were seen as enlightened beings, for example, Raja JANAK. The human AVATARS of VISHNU, RAMA and KRISHNA were also born into the *kshatriya varna* and ruled as kings.

Kumbha Mela Probably the largest religious gathering in the world, the festival is held every three years at the alternating sites of HARDWAR, Ujjain, Nasik and, finally, Allahabad where the YAMUNA and GANGA rivers meet. It is estimated that between twelve and twenty million pilgrims attended the last *mela* held in Allahabad in 1989, but this was surpassed by the festival held in 2001 where it was estimated that attendance could have been as high as fifty million. The festival celebrates the spilling of the jar of nectar of immortality at the creation of the universe. Too precious to be given over to the demons, VISHNU transported it to the realm of the gods. During the twelve year journey four drops of the nectar where spilled onto the four sites of the pilgrimage. One of the famous features of the festival is the procession in which all the major sects of Hinduism take part.

Kundalini *Lit. serpent power*. A Tantric concept that believes there are SIX CHAKRAS or concentrations of psychic power in the human body situated between the base of the spine and the top of the head. The *Kundalini* energy is normally quiescent in the *chakra* at the base of the spine. When awakened through certain practices it rises up like a serpent undulating through the chakras inside the SUSUMNA (a psychic canal that parallels the spinal cord) to the thousand petalled Lotus-*chakra* at the top of the head. Once the *Kundalini* energy reaches this point it is believed that SAMADHI takes place and liberation from SAMSARA can be achieved. (*See also* KUNDALINI YOGA; TANTRA)

Kundalini Yoga   A tantric system of YOGA that provides various MANTRAS, postures and breathing exercises believed to raise the KUNDALINI energy from its quiescent position at the base of the spine. *Kundalini yoga* attempts to unite the power of SHAKTI manifested as *Kundalini* with SHIVA, present as the ultimate existence in the lotus CHAKRA at the top of the head. The union of the two spiritual powers brings about a loss of duality and thus leads to liberation. As well as leading to liberation, it is believed that the awakened *Kundalini* power can result in super-natural prescience and a variety of miraculous powers. (*See also* SIDHHI; TANTRA)

Kurma   The AVATAR (manifestation) of VISHNU as a tortoise at the beginning of creation when the gods and demons churned the ocean of life. The divine tortoise appeared to churn the ocean in order for its secret treasures, such as the urn containing the nectar of immortality and the Goddess Lakshmi, to appear.

Kurma Purana   The PURANA or popular SMRITI scripure that tells the legends of the manifestation of VISHNU as KURMA, the tortoise-AVATAR.

Kurukshetra   The battle between the PANDAVAS and the Kauravas which is the subject matter of the MAHABHARATA. It is the famous location for the discourse between KRISHNA and ARJUNA recorded in the BHAGAVAD GITA.

L

Lakshman   The loyal and dedicated brother of RAMA who accompanies the AVATAR of VISHNU into exile along with Rama's wife, SITA. The two brothers spend fourteen years in exile in the forest and, after Sita's kidnapping by the demon king RAVANA, Lakshman went on to perform many great deeds of heroism. He is represented in Hindu temples as a young warrior standing with a bow next to the enthroned Rama and his consort Sita. (*See also* RAMAYANA)

Lakshmi   The consort of VISHNU who incarnates with his AVATARS and therefore the consorts of RAMA and KRISHNA, namely SITA and RADHA, are considered to be her manifestations. She is also the primordial GURU, the merciful form of the Goddess known as SRI. Usually found depicted as the loving and loyal consort of Vishnu in his temples, she also appears in her own right as the Goddess of wealth and fortune. Her image is often found in shops, places of business, offices and schools. Her festival is the well-known DIVALI or festival of lights that is celebrated throughout India in November and October, when businessmen will balance their books hoping for her blessings. Lakshmi is usually represented as a four-armed woman dressed in a red sari standing upon a lotus surrounded by water. Two of her arms hold lotus flowers but another arm showers gold coins.

Laws of Manu   The translation of *Manusmriti*, the famous text of BRAHMIN orthodoxy that focuses on the social prescriptions of DHARMA and outlines the duties of the ideal representative of each VARNA. Written somewhere between 300 BCE and 100 CE, it is the first text to insist that *varna* ascription is determined by birth. (*See also* MANU)

Laya yoga A system of YOGA that concentrates on techniques that achieve the dissolution of the self through absorption back into the Absolute. The practices are usually similar to TANTRA.

Lila The divine play or sport. In VEDANTA philosophy, the cosmos is created through the *lila* of the supreme being. It also describes the involvement of the supreme being in creation. This may be used to describe God's immanence or alternatively to express a series of inexplicable events that are ascribed to divine intervention in human affairs. In the Vaishnava tradition, *lila* is often used to describe the events in the life of an AVATAR of VISHNU. For example, it is used to describe the teasing play of love between Krishna and the GOPIS (shepherds and shepherdesses who adored him). (*See also* VAISHNAVISM)

Lingam A common phallus structure used to worship SHIVA. It is usually a U-shaped upright stone standing in the middle of a shallow teardrop-shaped bowl that represents the female sex organs (YONI). The *lingam* and the *yoni* represent the union of SHAKTI and Shiva, the male and the female principles of divine energy. The *lingam* can be found throughout India in countless places including village shrines, roadside shrines and great temples. Most Hindu temples in Britain contain a *lingam* which devotees cover in milk as a traditional form of worship.

Lobha The vice of greed that along with MOHA (delusion) and KRODHA (anger) is considered to be the root of all vices.

Madhva (1238–1317) A dualistic VAISHNAVITE from South India who opposed the ADVAITA VEDANTA of SHANKARA. Madhva's doctrine of DVAITA VEDANTA directly challenges Shankara's complete identification of ATMAN and BRAHMAN. Although the *atman* is completely dependent on God and shares in the nature of SATCHITANAND (truth, consciousness, bliss) that are the qualities of the divine being, individual souls remain eternally independent. The soul is therefore independent from both Brahman and the creation. The way to liberation is through complete self-surrender to VISHNU achieved through complete worship of the MURTI (image). Liberation is dependent on Vishnu's grace. However, Madhva's insistence on complete individuality of the JIVATMAN led to the possibility of separate eternal destinies. Thus he is the only famous Hindu philosopher to posit the destiny of everlasting hell. For this reason, it is sometimes suggested that he was influenced by the teachings of Christianity. Madhva was a prolific writer and commentator on scripture. His most famous work was the Brahma *Sutra-bhasya* but he also wrote famous commentaries on the BHAGAVAD GITA, the UPANISHADS, the RIG VEDA and the MAHABHARATA. His revolutionary contribution to the interpretation of the relationship between Brahman and *atman* lies in his interpretation of TAT TVAM ASI ('you are That'), the famous statement of the *Upanishads*. Madhva manipulates the order of the Sanskrit to arrive at the opposite meaning – That you are not – and then develops his ideas of dualism. (*See also* RAMANUJA; VAISHNAVISM)

Madya   Alcohol; one of the five MAKARAS forbidden to orthodox Hindus but used as a religious practice by those who follow the left-hand path of Tantric or SHAKTI cults. (*See also* TANTRA)

Mahabharata   The Sanskrit epic poem and part of the collection of SMRITI scripture that was completed around 200 CE. It contains nearly 100,000 verses that tell of the events which brought about the war between the PANDAVAS and Kauravas over ownership of a kingdom which culminated in the Battle of KURUKSHETRA. The famous discourse between KRISHNA and ARJUNA, that is the independent scripture, the BHAGAVAD GITA, is a part of the *Mahabharata*. Like many Hindu epics it ranges across many lifetimes showing how all the characters were inexorably led by KARMA throughout various rebirths to the eventual battle that took place. The *Mahabharata* is important as it develops the figures of VISHNU and SHIVA more fully for the first time. However, it is Vishnu in all his forms that becomes the central figure of the text and thus the scripture is essential to VAISHNAVITES and contains many of their doctrinal beliefs. The epic poem is very popular and is performed throughout India in various forms such as theatre, dance, puppet shows, cinema and most recently as 94 episodes on television. (*See also* VAISHNAVISM)

Mahadeva   *Lit. the great god*. Although one of the well-known appellations for SHIVA, it was originally used to describe RUDRA, the ancient deity first mentioned in the Rig Veda.

Mahant   Commonly used as a title for the head of a religious sect or the senior monk in charge of an ASHRAM or religious community. Historically the term was used in Sikhism during the period that the UDASIS, an ascetic group, were in control of the sacred sites in Amritsar. The Udasis used the title for the appointed custodians of Sikh gurdwaras.

Mahapuranas   The eighteen PURANAS that form part of accepted SMRITI scriptures used by major Hindu traditions. They are the bedrock of popular Hinduism as they provide the legends of most commonly worshipped deities. The *Puranas* also deal with themes that form

essential components of Hindu belief such as creation myths, dissolution myths, religious observances, pilgrimage places, liberation and
world cycles. Although not usually considered part of SHRUTI or Vedic
literature, they are nevertheless respected and tradition allocates their
authorship to the great sage, VYASA. The major *Puranas* are the *Vishnu
Purana, Brahma Purana, Padma Purana, Agni Purana, Varaha Purana,
Vamana Purana, Matsya Purana, Bhagavata Purana, Naradiya
Purana, Garuda Purana, Brahmanda Purana, Brahmavaivarta Purana,
Markandeya Purana, Bhavisya Purana, Shiva Purana, Linga Purana,
Skanda Purana, Kurma Purana.*

Mahat   According to SAMKHYA philosophy, *Mahat* is the Great Principle
that gives rise to individual existence; it is also known as BUDDHI, the
primordial intellect. *Mahat* is not God, but is itself a product of the
disturbance of the balance of the three GUNAS under the influence of
PURUSHA. (*See also* PRAKRITI)

Mahatma   *Lit. a great soul or great-souled one.* It is a title often
conferred on religious leaders or SANNYASIN monks. It was given to
GANDHI in recognition of his saintly qualities. It is sometimes used to
refer to the great spiritual figures in Hindu history.

Mahatmyas   A passage praising the greatness of each PURANA and
usually written at the beginning of each one as a prologue. They
usually indicate the manifold blessings that will come from either
reading the texts or even keeping a copy in the home.

Mahavakyas   A great saying or aphorism from a Vedic scriptural text.
The most famous is 'TAT TVAM ASI' or 'that art thou' from the
CHANDOGYA UPANISHAD that becomes the foundation for the various
interpretations of VEDANTA.

Mahayogi   *Lit. the great yogi.* Usually used as a name for SHIVA who is
regarded as the ultimate renunciate and the inspiration of many
Shaivite yogic orders. Contemporary YOGIS from the Shaivite tradition
may be given the honorific of *Mahayogi*.

Mahesh Yogi Maharishi   The founder of Transcendental Meditation Society better known in the West as TM. Mahesh Yogi became famous in the early 1960s when he first arrived in the West from his home in Rishikesh and attracted several famous stars of the entertainment world, including the Beatles. His movement has been very successful in attracting Westerners and teaching them basic MANTRA meditation. Recently the followers of TM have attracted considerable publicity over their claims to teach levitation.

Maithuna   Sexual intercourse outside of marriage; one of the five MAKARAS forbidden to orthodox Hindus but used a religious practice by those who follow the left-hand path of Tantric or SHAKTI cults. (*See also* TANTRA; VAMACHARIS)

Maitri Upanishad   One of the later *Upanishads* that attempts to synthesize Vedic teaching with other systems of thought and practice that had developed. One of these was YOGA, a set of mental and physical disciplines usually associated with SAMKHYA philosophy. The *Maitri Upanishad* uses the categories of yogic discipline such as DHYANA (meditation), *dharana* (concentration) and SAMADHI (absorption) in order to discuss liberation, or union of the Self with BRAHMAN.

Makaras   The five forbidden or taboo practices that are used by the followers of the left-hand path of TANTRA as religious or spiritual disciplines. They are drinking alcohol, eating meat, unlawful sexual intercourse, eating fish, and eating fried rice. Left-hand Tantra reverses the normal Hindu conception of auspiciousness or purity in order to remove the problem of attachment by indulging under controlled conditions in the vices that normally lead to worldly attachment or pollution. The five forbidden substances would be taken after repetition of holy MANTRAS and under the guidance of a GURU. (*See also* MADYA; MAITHUNA; MAMSA; MATSYA; MUDRA; VAMACHARIS)

Mala   A rosary or circle of stringed beads used in repeating MANTRAS, traditionally made from tulsi or sandalwood. The term is also used for a garland placed around the neck of a holy person or dignitary.

Mamsa Eating meat; one of the five MAKARAS forbidden to orthodox Hindus but used as a religious practice by those who follow the left-hand path of *Tantric* or SHAKTI cults. (*See also* TANTRA; VAMACHARIS)

Manas / Man Although used in most of the six schools of orthodox Hindu philosophy, the meaning is slightly different. The BRHADARANYAKA UPANISHAD describes *manas* as the attached mind and it is this meaning that becomes developed in mediaeval BHAKTI and SANT traditions. This carries through into modern Hinduism where it is usually used to describe the aspect of mind that can lead a person away from truth or knowledge of God. It was commonly used by mediaeval *Bhakti sants* like KABIR and Nanak to describe the mind deluded by anger, greed, hatred, lust and attachment. In meditation, it is the *manas* which prevents the ability to experience ATMAN or BRAHMAN. ADVAITA VEDANTA refers to the sense that co-ordinates the perceptions of the other five senses and differentiates between subject and object, and thus holds the *atman* under the spell of illusion. (*See also* MAYA)

Mandala A symbolic diagram circular in form that represents wholeness or completeness. It is often used to represent the cosmos or the totality of SAMSARA. In some traditions such as TANTRA, it is used as visual meditation aid.

Mandapa The rectangular hall usually supported by pillars that constitutes the part of a temple used by the worshippers. (*See also* MANDIR)

Mandir A Hindu temple that contains an image (MURTI) of a god or goddess. Temples in India range from huge complexes to small roadside shrines, but the traditional pattern for all larger temples is an inner sanctum containing the image, usually oblong or square in shape. This consecrated area is covered by a tapering tower or spire and is known as the *vimana*. The BRAHMIN priests will stay in this area to serve the deity and perform the various rituals. The devotees will remain on the other side of this consecrated area except for when receiving DARSHAN (blessings) of the *murti*. This assembly area may be roofed and pillared. Larger temples may contain living quarters, kitchens, store-rooms, and subsidiary shrines to divine consorts or lesser deities associated with the major temple deity. Some temples can be very large and ornate and in the South consist of concentric squares each containing deities. The main deity will be in the central square. (*See also* GARBHA-GRIHA; SHIKHARA)

Mantra A Sanskrit sacred formula or chant usually consisting of the names or attributes of a deity. It may also be a verse from scripture. From very early times, sound was a fundamental aspect of the Vedic sacrifice performed by BRAHMINS. Many Vedic hymns are composed of short sentences in praise of the deity and these became well-known *mantras* or formulations of truth in the form of sound. In other words, *mantras* are considered to bring into reality the special power of the deity through the use of spoken speech in much the same way as the MURTI itself can work through the sense of sight. *Mantras* are used to facilitate worship or as a meditation practice to control the mind through their continuous repetition. A *mantra* may be bestowed with magical qualities that allow the desires of the devotee to be fulfilled through repetition. A *mantra* is usually provided by a GURU on initiation and the disciple is instructed in the duration and number of repetitions. (*See also* MANAS)

Manu The founder of the human race, or primal man, and the Hindu lawgiver. He is believed to have provided the rules of conduct (DHARMA) followed in Hinduism. These are found in the 'LAWS OF MANU' and because Manu is the mythical father of the human race his ordinances are perceived as universal or natural.

Marga A path leading to salvation sometimes used as synonymous with religion. There are three basic paths in Hinduism that incorporate the complete range of traditions within their all-embracing fold. These are KARMA YOGA, JNANA YOGA and BHAKTI YOGA; the paths of action, knowledge and devotion.

Mata Independent female DEVATAS, rather than the great goddesses of the SHAKTI tradition, found in village or rural Hinduism. They often have specialist functions associated with particular diseases, and one of the most famous is the Goddess of Smallpox whose temple is even in VARANASI. New goddess cults continue to come into existence and recently a large following has appeared for Santoshi Mata, a previously little known goddess who may have first appeared in a popular film (*Shakti*).

Math / Matha   A monastic institution where large numbers of renunciates live together. The most famous are the four *maths* founded by SHANKARA in the four quarters of India. This was the first attempt to systematize Hindu renunciates into orders similar to those in Buddhism. The four *maths* continue as orthodox forms of Hindu renunciation and their respective leaders or Shankaracharyas are respected national religious figures. (*See also* ADVAITA VEDANTA)

Mathura   The ancient pilgrimage town associated with VISHNU believed to be the birthplace of KRISHNA and situated in North India near to VRINDAVAN on the Jumna river. The original legends of Krishna place his birth at Dvarka in Gujarat. However, it is possible that the new site at Mathura could have been adopted after the discovery of Vrindavan by CAITANYA in the thirteenth century as the site of Krishna's exile and life with the GOPIS. The temple that celebrates Krishna's birthplace shares a wall with an historic mosque and is therefore guarded by troops to avoid a similar incident to that at the Babri mosque in AYODHYA, which was disputed sacred territory and destroyed by zealous Hindus.

Matsya   The first AVATAR of VISHNU who manifested as a giant fish to save MANU, the primordial man, from the primeval flood.

Maya   Usually translated as illusion, but various schools of thought amongst Hindu sects and schools of philosophy have different understandings of the concept. All Hindus agree that illusion is the power that prevents or obscures the vision or apprehension of ultimate reality, but the nature of illusion is debated. Essentially, the difference falls into two categories: those that believe *maya* is a human creation and those that believe it is a divine creation. *Maya* can be perceived as caused by the soul identifying itself with mind and matter, thereby forgetting its true nature. Or it can be seen as the divine power that creates the universe as appearance and obscures the reality of the ultimate being, BRAHMAN. In this sense, *maya* can also mean the actual creative power of the supreme being and is then associated with SHAKTI, the female creative principle. Sometimes, Hindus will use *maya* to mean delusion rather than illusion; for example, the attraction to certain sensual pleasures will be described as *maya*. Whatever the particular interpretation, the concept of *maya* is central to understanding the Hindu world-view, as liberation from SAMSARA cannot be obtained without overcoming the illusionary power of *maya*. If *maya* is a human creation then the potential for self-liberation exists in human spiritual effort alone, but if *maya* is a divine creation, then grace will be required to be liberated. (*See also* MUKTI)

Mayin   The supreme being or BRAHMAN described as the originator of MAYA or illusion.

Mimansa   One of the six orthodox schools of philosophy that all recognize the authority of the VEDAS. Mimansa or Purva Mimansa is concerned with the ritual dimension of the Vedic texts and has developed a theology based on Vedic aphorisms or ritual formulas. Those who developed Mimansa assumed without question that the Brahminic or Vedic sacrifice was the means to attain all divine favours and correct performance was essential. Consequently Mimansa continues to be concerned with DHARMA or correct performance of action. It is therefore a path for the twice-born VARNAS and it excludes SUDRAS and women. The goal of Mimansa is the attainment of heaven and originally it was not theistic since both earth and the *Vedas* were deemed to be eternal. Later it developed into a theistic system, probably under the influence of the various forms of VEDANTA that were so successful in gaining adherents from all classes of Hindus. The primary scripture for the Mimansa school is the Mimansa SUTRA written around 200 BCE. (*See also* DARSHANA)

Mirabhai   The most famous female devotee of Northern India. She was born in 1547 and is believed to have fallen in love with KRISHNA at an early age. She betrothed herself to the deity and adorned, bathed, sang and danced to the image of Krishna. Later she was married to the ruler of Chitor, a family who traditionally worshipped the Goddess. Mirabhai's continuous devotions to the image of Krishna contained in the local temple were mistakenly believed to be an adulterous relationship. Her husband broke into the temple only to find her singing love songs, enraptured before Krishna's image. It is believed that the Emperor Akbar travelled incognito to hear her songs of devotion. She was ordered to leave the kingdom and settled in VRINDAVAN where her fame spread throughout North India. She began to identify herself with RADHA, the consort of Krishna. She eventually returned to her husband's court but after his death, Mira's mother-in-law continued to persecute her so she again retired to Vrindavan. It is believed that she died in the city through being absorbed back into Krishna's form in the temple. This form of death is a rare honour bestowed on very few of Hinduism's countless lovers of the divine. Mirabhai is remembered throughout Northern India as the embodiment of devotion and her thousands of songs are still recorded by modern artistes and sung on radio as well as in congregational worship. Some traditions believe that in later life she became a disciple of the low-caste SANT master, RAVIDAS. (*See also* BHAKTI)

Mitra   A Vedic god associated with the sun. He is the ruler of the day and a close associate of VARUNA, the guardian of cosmic order. He was regarded as a benefactor and close friend to human beings. (*See also* SAVITRI; SURYA)

Moha   Delusion. One of the three vices, along with (LOBHA) greed and (KRODHA) anger, identified as the source of all evil. *Moha* is identified as the key to all vice as it is believed that greed and anger arise from it. Delusion is associated with unconsciousness or ignorance which manifests as carelessness, misjudgement, false pride and confusion. When overtaken by unconsciousness or in a condition of ignorance, the human being falls prey to the other vices through the loss of discrimination and self-control. (*See also* MAYA)

Mohenjodaro   The city excavated in the first half of the twentieth century along with HARAPPA and originally believed to confirm the theory that the DRAVIDIAN or Harappan culture was destroyed suddenly by an invasion of the ARYANS from the North-West. The theory is now under challenge but remains speculative. The script of the two cities remains undeciphered and theories concerning religion and its relationship to the development of Hinduism rely on interpretation of discovered artifacts.

Moksha The end goal of most forms of the Hindu spiritual quest. It refers to release of the soul from SAMSARA or the cycle of rebirth and is usually translated as liberation. It can be achieved by following one of the three MARGAS or paths to liberation. The various schools of philosophy offer variations on the concept of *moksha* depending on how they regard the relationship of BRAHMAN, the Absolute Being, and ATMAN, the eternal in human beings. For ADVAITA VEDANTINS, liberation is the realization that Brahman and *atman* are identical. For most BHAKTI or devotional traditions, liberation is perceived as eternal companionship with the Divine, usually as a form of VISHNU. The many SAMPRADAYAS or sects of Hinduism offer a vast variety of methods for achieving liberation but there is a basic distinction between those that consider liberation to be ultimately achievable only after death and those that believe that liberation is obtainable whilst alive as a human being. Release from *samsara* results in freedom from all suffering and the enjoyment of the qualities of Brahman described as SATCHITANANDA, or Truth, Consciousness and Bliss. (*See also* VEDANTA)

Mrtyu Death; in the PURANAS, Mrtyu is said to have been born from the offspring of DHARMA and Adharma, who were in turn the grand-children of BRAHMA's offspring, the primeval man or MANU. *Mrtyu* is still prayed to at funerals by contemporary Hindus as the Lord of Cremation.

Mudra Eating fried rice; one of the five MAKARAS forbidden to orthodox Hindus but indulged by those who follow the left-hand path of Tantric or SHAKTI cults. More commonly, *mudra* refers to the sophisticated symbolic language formed by hand gestures used in various dance forms but also as a symbolic language used in YOGA postures. Various deities and representations of holy people are often depicted with their hands in various *mudras*. The most common are the *abhaya mudra*, expressing tranquility or protection, where the hand is turned to the front with the fingers pointing upwards and the *varada mudra*, expressing blessings, where the hand is turned to the front but the fingers point downwards. TANTRA has developed these into a very sophisticated system and they are also used extensively in some forms of Buddhism. (*See also* VAMACHARIS)

Mukti An alternative term for liberation from the endless cycle of birth and rebirth otherwise known as MOKSHA.

Mundaka Upanishad One of the principal UPANISHADS, which introduces the theme of higher and lower knowledge. Lower knowledge consists of the study of scripture, including the VEDAS, but higher knowledge is the direct perception or 'grasping' of the imperishable BRAHMAN.

Mundan Head-shaving ceremony performed as a rite of passage in the first or third year of life. (*See also* SAMSKAR)

Murti The image of a deity used as a focus of worship either installed in a temple or at home. The power of the deity is believed to exist within the installed image and a temple deity is consecrated in a ceremony where life is believed to be breathed into the MURTI. Hinduism contains a vast array of deities: human, supernatural beings, animal, half-human, half-animal, all both male and female. The most important are the forms of SHIVA and VISHNU and their family members. These two deities make up the dominant traditions of SHAIVISM and VAISHNAVISM. However, Hindus generally believe that all the deities are manifestations or aspects of the one Absolute Being, BRAHMAN who pervades the universe. Hindus will choose their deity according to need, caste, status or sectarian allegiance. Although the focus will be on the chosen deity there is no denial of the others in the Hindu pantheon. Thus Hinduism cannot strictly be defined as polytheism; henotheism would be a more accurate description of MURTI worship.

Murugan An ancient deity of the Tamils, associated with youth, beauty and freedom, and still popularly worshipped throughout Tamil-speaking

South India. According to ancient Tamil texts, he is the god of war whose emblems are the elephant and the blue-feathered peacock. The usual form of worship involves offerings of rice and honey, but goats are also sacrificed. His temples or pilgrimage places are usually on high places. Murugan worship has been identified with the North Indian worship of SKANDA, the ARYAN god of war. Since Skanda has become identified with KARTIKEYA, the multi-headed son of SHIVA, Murugan has been assimilated into SHAIVISM, the worship of Shiva and his family. A further assimilation has resulted in the merging of Murugan's identity with SUBRAMANIYAM.

Mushaka The rat sanctified as the vehicle of GANESH. There are temples in India that are sacred to rats. In VRINDAVAN, there is an annual procession where an especially fattened and large rat is taken through the city as a representative of the animal's sanctity.

N

Nagas A collective name for various groups of renunciates, usually from the Shaivite tradition, who are famous for their lack of clothing. Some Nagas are fully naked but others wear a small loincloth. Their hair is worn long in locks and they cover their bodies in ash, their foreheads and limbs are usually covered in painted sectarian marks. Although Hindu renunciates are often associated with tranquility and non-violence, the various Naga groups formed armed bands, probably in order to resist attack by Muslims. However, they have been known to fight each other. A well-known group of Nagas is the NATH YOGIS or KANPHATAS. (*See also* SHAIVISM)

Nagas Mythical snake-gods that dwell in the netherworlds, often represented as cobras with several heads. Snakes, particularly cobras, are regarded as a sacred animal. (*See also* SESA)

Najar / Nazar The evil eye; believed to be incurred by the envy of neighbours or supernatural beings. In village Hinduism, severe and recurring misfortune could be interpreted as some form of malevolent possession, the most common of which is the evil eye. As in most cases of possession, the cure would be sought with a local practitioner. (*See also* OJHA)

Namajapa The remembrance of the Name or Names of God. Although reference to the remembrance of God's Name is found in many ancient Hindu scriptures, it is the mediaeval BHAKTI tradition which brings the practice to popularity amongst the masses. The great bhakti poets of both SHAIVISM and VAISHNAVISM praise the Name of God in their poems. Generally, the practice consists of the repetition of a favoured name of the deity of a particular SAMPRADAYA (sect) often aided by use of a MALA (rosary). The success of the bhakti tradition has led to a proliferation of divine names and the composition of litanies containing the thousand names of God. The most popular names are those associated with VISHNU, SHIVA and the DEVI. The Hindu scriptures state that to be effective, the Name of God has to be the Name that God acknowledges to be His eternal Name and therefore identical to Himself. It is stated that this remembrance or repetition of this eternal or uncreated Name is the only means of salvation. Many *bhakti* and SANT poets stated that this Name could only be known through association and initiation with a SATGURU (true GURU). This particular belief was developed by the Sikhs to become a new religion based around the *Satguru* and the SATNAM. (*See also* SABDA)

Namarupa   *Lit. Name and form.* TULSIDAS wrote a famous passage in the RAMACHARITAMANASA in which he argues that the Name of God is greater than both the absolute BRAHMAN and the various ISHWARAS or AVATARS (forms or incarnations of God). Tulsidas's argument is that Brahman, the repository of infinite truth, consciousness and bliss, dwells in all hearts, but still creatures are miserable; yet by the remembrance of the Name they become joyful. He goes on to argue that AVATARS only save favoured devotees at a particular time or place but that the remembrance of the Name of God has saved countless souls since the beginning of time. Tulsidas does, however, acknowledge that Name and Form are one entity, and cannot be separated from each other. (*See also* NAMAJAPA; NIRGUNA BRAHMAN; SAGUNA BRAHMAN)

Namaskar   The typical Hindu greeting made to each other and on greeting a deity. The hands are folded together in a prayer position, the head is bowed and a greeting will be made with the words *Namaskar* or *Namaste*, but particular religious sects (SAMPRADAYAS) may have their own unique wording often associated with the particular name of their chosen deity.

Namdev A fourteenth-century SANT, a tailor by trade, who taught that caste was not a barrier to complete devotion to God. As with most *sant* teachers, Namdev focused on remembrance of the Name of God to attain salvation, taught and wrote his poetry in the vernacular, and preached that God can be found within the heart of the devotee regardless of caste, creed or gender. (*See also* NAMAJAPA)

Nandi The bull, sacred as the vehicle (VAHANA) of SHIVA and whose statues are found in front of the entrance of Shiva temples. Some statues of Nandi are massive.

Narada Devi The wife of RAMAKRISHNA Paramhansa. She was married to him as a child and the relationship was never consummated. Narada Devi joined him at the temple in Dakshineshwar in 1871 as a devotee. He regarded her as a manifestation of the Goddess but probably not in any significant sense other than his ecstatic ability to see the Divine in all. However, after his death some followers began to regard her as an incarnation of the Goddess.

Narasimha The fourth incarnation (AVATAR) of VISHNU who manifested as half-man, half-lion to destroy the demon HIRANYAKASHIPU, the father and persecutor of the child-devotee PRAHLAD.

Narayan One of the most common names for invoking VISHNU. The earliest mention of Narayan in Hindu scripture is in the *Satapatha Brahmana*, a part of the Vedic texts that states that Purusa Narayan performed a five-day sacrifice to become the Lord of Creation. In one of the Vedic forest texts, the *Taittiriya Aranyaka*, Narayan is referred to as the supreme Lord of Creation and identified with HARI, the other common appellation of Vishnu. The same text identifies Narayan with Vishnu.

Nastika Any of the unorthodox schools of Hindu philosophy that do not accept the Vedic revelation or their authority. Principally, these are considered to be Buddhism and Jainism that went on to become religions in their own right. Sikhs also do not base authority on the teachings of the VEDAS. There were other groups in antiquity, such as the atheistic Charvakas and the extreme ascetics, the Ajivikas, that denied the Vedic revelation but these have disappeared. (*See also* ASTIKA; DARSHANA)

Nataraja SHIVA as the Lord of the Dance who controls the movement of the cosmos and orders destruction. Nataraja is depicted as an ascetic with one head but four arms. One hand holds a small drum maintaining the rhythm of the universe and the other contains the fire of destruction. The other two hands are kept in the MUDRAS (symbolic gestures) of salvation and protection. He dances on the demon of ignorance and is surrounded by a circle representing an arch of flames that signify the cycle of life or time.

Natchiketas The young BRAHMIN boy who is sacrificed to Death by his father in the KATHA UPANISHAD. Because Death does not receive him at the gates of the otherworld, he is offered three boons after waiting for three days. As a result of this a discourse takes place between Death and Natchiketas on the nature of Truth. This discourse is one of the most famous in the UPANISHADS and tells of the relationship between BRAHMAN and ATMAN and how liberation can be achieved. Effectively the *Upanishad* uses the literary device of making Death the teacher of the young *brahmin* disciple.

Nath yogis A vast variety of both renunciate and married orders of YOGIS who claim that their teachings are derived from GORAKHNATH and his guru, Matsyendranath. Many of the orders have become semi-nomadic sub-castes who survive through fortune-telling, supernatural cures, exorcisms and snake charming. (*See also* KANPHATA)

Navaratri An important festival to the Goddess DURGA or Amba celebrated for nine nights in September/October. The festival commemorates the victory of the Goddess over the buffalo-demon, Mahishasura, the king of demons and embodiment of ignorance and chaos. The demon-king had thrown the gods out of heaven and taken up residence there himself. Cosmic order had been thrown upside down, and Durga's victory restored DHARMA. The tenth day of the festival is known as DASSERA or victory. Sometimes the complete festival of ten days is known as Dassera. The festival also coincides with RAMLILA, the re-enacting of the victory of RAMA over RAVANA, the demon king of Sri Lanka, and therefore both are often celebrated together, especially in North India. Navaratri is an important festival for the Gujarati Hindu community in Britain as they have strong traditions of Durga worship, but the Goddess is known as Amba.

Nayanars Sixty-three SHIVA BHAKTI teachers from South India who composed many hymns and poems in praise of the deity from the seventh to tenth centuries CE. As with many later mediaeval *bhakti* groups, the Nayanars taught that caste was irrelevant to devotion and that repetition of the Name of God was the only means to salvation in the KALI YUGA (Age of Darkness). The Nayanars taught the doctrine of eternal separation from God in order to experience the fruits of the relationship of blissful devotion and the showering of Divine Grace. Their poems were kept in several collections that were combined in the tenth century to form the major Shaivite scripture of Tamil-speaking India, the Tirumurai. (*See also* ALVARS; SHAIVISM)

Nazar *See* NAJAR.

Neti, Neti *Lit.* 'Not this, not this'. The negative term used to answer enquiries concerning the reality or nature of BRAHMAN in some of the UPANISHADS. As an impersonal Absolute devoid of form or qualities, Brahman was considered to be indescribable and beyond the conception of the intellect. Even though Hindu sages acknowledge the ability of the human being to directly experience absorption into Brahman through various paths, they also agree that even the person who had achieved such an experience would not be able to describe it. (*See also* SAMADHI)

Nirguna Formless, without attributes or qualities. The doctrine of the formless, impersonal BRAHMAN was most fully formulated in the teachings of ADVAITA VEDANTA by SHANKARA. The basic division in the mediaeval BHAKTI tradition is between those that worship through a form of God or ISHWARA, and those that worship the formless God (*See also* NAMARUPA; SAGUNA; SANT).

Nirguna Bhakti   A term used to describe intense devotion to the formless God without the worship of an ISHWARA or an AVATAR. This tradition, often classified as SANT, developed in North India during the mediaeval period and is represented by such figures as KABIR and Nanak. It is often suggested that such devotion to a formless God developed under the influence of Islam but the teachings are already existent within Hinduism and found in the UPANISHADS. However, the application of qualities to the formless BRAHMAN provided opportunities for synthesis with Islam especially in the Sufi tradition.

Nirguna Brahman   The term for the formless BRAHMAN without attributes or qualities. However, even the formless Brahman is usually described as SATCHITANANDA (truth, consciousness, bliss). The main division in Hindu religious thought concerns the order of divine emanation. Those that promote the form of God as supreme, for example, VAISHNAVITE sects, do not deny the formlessness of Brahman, however, they perceive the formless as an emanation of the eternal form. ADVAITA VEDANTINS do not deny the forms of the Divine but rather see them as temporary manifestations of the formless. The debate between these two schools can at times become heated. (*See also* RAMANUJA; SHANKARA; VAISHNAVISM)

Nirvana   The cessation of the wheel of existence and the end of SAMSARA. More common in Buddhism but sometimes used in Hinduism to describe MOKSHA or MUKTI.

Nishkarm karma   The practice of performing action without concern over or attachment to the results of the action. In this way, the BHAGAVAD GITA claims that it is possible to maintain complete tranquility without physical renunciation. The teachings of the *Bhagavad Gita* define renunciation of the fruits of action as KARMA YOGA, leading to liberation through absence of desire when performing actions.

Niyama   The second of the eight stages on the path to liberation as defined by the YOGA school of philosophy. *Niyama* refers to full observance of the rules associated with DHARMA and devotion to the Lord.

In particular it refers to cultivating observance of purity, contentment, austerity, study and dedicating one's actions to the Lord.

Nyasa A Tantric mental concentration using MANTRAS that is believed to place or 'project' certain divine powers or deities into parts of the body of the practitioner. (*See also* TANTRA)

Nyaya One of the six orthodox schools of Hindu philosophy that acknowledge the authority of the VEDAS. Its basic text is the *Nyaya Sutra* attributed to Gotama, the believed founder of the tradition, somewhere between 200 BCE and 200 CE. *Nyaya* lays stress on rational analysis of logical arguments and regards knowledge or right reasoning as the key to liberation. Ignorance is seen as the cause of suffering and bondage to the wheel of SAMSARA. *Nyaya* was not originally a theistic system but accepted the idea of God at a later date under the influence of SHAIVISM. The *Nyaya* School remains strong in the state of Bengal. (*See also* ASTIKA; DARSHANA)

O

Ojha A non-BRAHMIN village priest who functions as a shaman. He/she will be consulted in order to deal with possession by ghosts, demons, the evil eye and other supernatural beings that are believed to be the cause of human misfortune. (*See also* BHUT; NAJAR)

OM *See* AUM.

P

Padmasana The lotus position which is believed to be the best posture for meditation. Originally, the YOGA SUTRAS of PATANJALI recommended that postures (ASANAS) for meditation should be comfortable and relaxed, but a variety of more complex positions developed. The most famous is the *padmasana* and many depictions of Hindu gods and sages are shown in the well-known position where the legs are crossed with feet placed sole upwards on the opposite thigh.

Pancayat A traditional Hindu village council or caste assembly that functions to enforce caste regulations and resolve disagreements between caste members. Although Hinduism has no established criteria for orthodoxy that can be reinforced through a central authority, the leaders of the *pancayats* have traditionally maintained caste orthodoxy and morality, sometimes enforcing through imposition of penances or even expulsion from the community. (*See also* JATI)

Pancgavya The mixture of the five products (milk, yoghurt, butter, dung and urine) of the cow, an animal considered to be highly sacred, used as purification against ritual pollution. (*See also* PAP)

Panchamas *Lit. the fifth group*. A term for the castes outside of the four VARNAS. (*See also* HARIJANS)

Panchatantra A scripture consisting of a collection of fables, mainly all animal stories with a moral. The animals are depicted with virtues such as wisdom and loyalty.

Pandavas   Five brothers whose conflict over the ownership of their kingdom with their cousins, the Kauravas, culminated in the Battle of KURUKSHETRA. Their story is told in the great epic, the MAHABHARATA. The two principal brothers are the eldest, YUDHISHTHIRA, whose sense of justice is so revered that he is sometimes identified with Dharmraj, the King of Righteousness, and ARJUNA, the youngest. Arjuna becomes associated with devotion to KRISHNA as he is chosen to receive the great revelation of the BHAGAVAD GITA and the vision of Krishna's cosmic form.

Pandit   A title for a member of the *Brahmin* caste who performs a priestly function but specializes in the study and interpretation of scriptures, and ancient texts of law and philosophy. The term PANDIT is commonly used as a title for a learned man or a priest.

Pap / Papa   Sometimes translated as sin but more accurately as moral or natural evil. In Hindu texts, the term can be used to describe those that are ritually impure because they consciously persist in performing impure actions or because they have been unfortunate enough to be born into a ritually impure caste or even as a woman. This is attributed to wrongdoing in previous lives. A third meaning points to people who are wrongdoers in the more conventional sense of performing morally wrong actions or leading others into immorality. Strictly speaking, the best translation of *pap* as used in Sanskrit scriptures is demerit, a state caused by poor observance of traditional rituals, however, in common parlance, more and more Hindus are beginning to use it to refer to immorality. The opposite of *pap* is PUNYA (merit) and it is necessary to understand both in order to grasp the full concept.

Parashurama   The seventh AVATAR of VISHNU or RAMA of the Axe who incarnated to protect BRAHMINS from the tyranny of unjust KSHATRIYAS (warriors). It is said that Vishnu manifested in human form as the son of a brahmin but lived the lifestyle of *kshatriya* in order to rescue the brahmin caste from complete domination. In the RAMAYANA of TULSIDAS, he appears when Rama breaks the bow of SHIVA in order to win the hand of SITA in marriage. Parashurama is infuriated that the bow has been broken by two members of the *kshatriya* caste but is humiliated verbally by Rama and his brother, LAKSHMAN. This presents the odd dilemma of the seventh *avatar* being admonished by the eighth. However, Rama is a true or ideal *kshatriya* who protects the brahmins. As an incarnation of DHARMA, he is outraged by the mixing of VARNA functions manifested in Parashurama. The story demonstrates that a new age has arrived where brahmins no longer need to fear *kshatriya* domination. Parashurama, however, becomes the forerunner and prototype of martial renunciate sects in Hinduism. (*See also* NAGAS)

Paratantra The DVAITA VEDANTA doctrine taught by MADHVA that stated that all worldly things depend for their activity on God.

Parikrama A special pilgrimage around a sacred city that takes pilgrims on a prescribed route that visits all the holy places and important temples. (*See also* PRAVRAJYA)

Parivraka A Hindu pilgrim. (*See also* PRAVRAJYA)

Parvati One of the forms of Mahadevi, the Goddess and the principal consort of SHIVA. She is the Goddess of the Himalayas and also known as UMA or DEVI. The PURANAS and the RAMACHARITAMANASA of TULSIDAS provide a rich source of legends regarding the relationship of Shiva and Parvati, and his other consorts are usually considered to be her incarnations. In TANTRA she is identified with SHAKTI, the cosmic female power, and is considered to be so close to Shiva that they are inseparable as one composite being. She is also regarded as the mother of KARTIKEYA and GANESH, the elephant-headed god who is popularly worshipped throughout India.

Patanjali The reputed author of the YOGA SUTRAS and founder of the YOGA school of philosophy, one of the six Hindu orthodox schools, somewhere around the second century BCE.

Pinda An offering of ten balls of cooked rice, prepared on the eleventh day of a funeral period, which are believed to assist the deceased in finding a new and better rebirth. They are also prepared and given to guests and BRAHMIN priests at the auspicious SHRADDHA ceremony that takes place a year after the death and thereafter annually.

Pipal A sacred tree often used by renunciate monks to meditate under or as a site of a shrine. The leaves are also used in religious rituals as offerings to deities.

Pradakshina The common practice of circumambulating a shrine, always keeping the shrine itself on one's right. (*See also* DARSHAN; MANDIR; MURTI)

Pradakshina patha A path around the deity so that pilgrims or worshippers can circumambulate. (*See also* PRADAKSHINA)

Prahlad A legendary child devoted to VISHNU. He was the son of a demon king named HIRANYA KASIPU who thought that he was the supreme power in the world. His son refused to acknowledge his father as the supreme power and worshipped Vishnu. Consequently he suffered extreme persecution from his father but would never renounce his faith. Vishnu eventually incarnated in a lion/man (Nrisinha) form and destroyed Prahlad's father. The devotion of Prahlad is remembered in the HOLI festival. (*See also* HOLI; NARASIMHA)

Prajapati In the ancient Vedic tradition where the brahminic sacrificial ritual is described as the creator and preserver of the cosmic order, Prajapati is described as the Lord of Generation. The RIG VEDA identifies Prajapati with PURUSHA, the cosmic entity that creates the universe through a cosmic sacrificial act. Prajapati is then restored to life by AGNI, the god of fire. This restoration of Prajapati echoes the stages of the fire sacrifice, so important in brahminic ritual. The myth of Prajapati therefore provides an archetypal version of the most important Vedic ritual. (*See also* BRAHMIN; HAVAN)

Prakriti The basic substance of being or primordial matter that exists as latent energy but when empowered by contact with PURUSHA (the life-essence or spirit) gives rise to the differentiated material world that is experienced through the mind and senses. *Prakriti* consists of three

GUNAS: RAJAS, TAMAS, and SATTVA, that exist in an infinite variety of combinations to form all created beings. However, *prakriti* does not of itself contain consciousness which is only a quality of *purusha*. Once united with consciousness, experience is possible. However, mental and moral faculties are the creation of the *gunas* intermixing and are part of *prakriti*, not *purusha*. The dualistic theory of explaining animate and inanimate creation through two interwoven and eternal forces, known as *purusha* and *prakriti*, was first used by the non-theistic SAMKHYA school of philosophy but is now common throughout Hinduism, even in theistic systems.

Prana The breath of life that supports all other life functions. There is an ode to the breath of life in the RIG VEDA but later philosophical and YOGIC systems suggest that there are several vital functions or breaths. Many *yogic* systems are based on breathing or breath control. Certainly by the time of the UPANISHADS concentration on the breath as a means of controlling the senses was a well-developed system. (*See also* PRANAYAMA)

Pranam Prostration or obeisance to a deity, a GURU or even a respected elder. The physical action varies from simply folding hands and bowing the head to lying completely prostrate on the ground. More commonly, devotees may kneel with their heads on the ground. It is also common to touch or even kiss the feet of a holy person or an image. (*See also* NAMASKAR)

Pranayama *Lit. breath restraint.* There are various ancient methods of controlling the breath used in Hinduism either to control the mind or achieve spiritual states. The most common is slow deep breathing through the nose where the inhaling and exhaling is increasingly prolonged until the breathing is hardly existent. It is claimed that some YOGIS can suspend their breath completely. Other methods of *pranayama* involve suppression of the breath, different rhythms of breathing and sometimes violent inhalations or exhalations. All *pranayama* systems are explained as methods to assist mind control and one-pointed concentration, hopefully leading to the desired state of ego-loss known as SAMADHI. The main object of *pranayama* is

PRATYAHARA or withdrawal of the senses inwards and away from the outer world. *Pranayama* is the fourth stage of the path of YOGA as explained in the classical texts of the school. (*See also* PRANA)

Prasada Food offered to a deity or a guru which is then considered to be consecrated and is shared out amongst the devotees. In temple worship the *prasada* is usually offered to the devotees after the ceremony of ARTI at the conclusion of the ritual or PUJA (worship). *Prasada* is offered to the deity in two ways: devotees will bring offerings with them which are distributed; or the deity is offered food by the priests at the normal times of eating. This is also distributed or eaten by the priests themselves. *Prasada* can also refer to the blessings or grace of the divinity which is also considered to be a gift from the Divine. (*See also* MURTI)

Pratyahara Explained in the YOGA SUTRAS as withdrawal of the senses from their objects, or the state of being where the senses no longer have contact with the outer world. This is a desired state in most meditation systems. The achievement of *pratyahara* is the fifth stage of the path of YOGA as explained in the classical texts of the school. (*See also* PATANJALI; PRANAYAMA; SAMADHI)

Pravachan A type of religious lecture based on recitation and interpretation of passages from any scripture.

Pravrajya Sanskrit for a pilgrimage. The spiritual map of India contains countless pilgrimage sites that range from local shrines to all-India sites visited by millions annually. Many Hindus perform pilgrimage and abandon their normal everyday life for a period of time which is used to seek moral and spiritual benefits from a sacred space. There are many famous pilgrimage towns and sites on riverbanks and some pilgrimages link various sites. Such pilgrimages may take three months and involve the pilgrim in hundreds of miles of traveling. The more difficult the pilgrimage in terms of hardship, the more merit is acquired by the pilgrim. (*See also* PARIKRAMA; PRADAKSHINA)

Preta From the day of death to around two or three weeks later the deceased person is considered to be ghost (*preta*). The correct rituals have to be performed by relatives to build up the soul so that it can leave the earth and go on to its next existence. For a variety of reasons a soul can remain earthbound as a ghost, particularly if the correct rituals are not performed. In this case, the *preta* or ghost is likely to cause problems, especially for relatives, until exorcized by an expert in the art. (*See also* OJHA; PINDA; SHRADDHA)

Puja Hindu worship. All rituals and ceremonies of worship are generically called *puja* but the term is commonly used to describe rituals performed to a deity or a GURU either in the home or at the temple. Individuals will visit a temple or shrine and offer flowers, fruit, money, rice, grains and prayers to the MURTI (deity). In the home, families will perform *puja* in a small shrine maintained in the house. This could take place twice a day but more often in the morning. When puja is performed congregationally at a temple, a BRAHMIN priest will usually oversee the event and lead the prayers. The priest himself will perform specialist *pujas* to the *murtis* in his temple particularly at dawn and nighttime. The *murtis* are awoken with special ceremonies and offerings. At night they are put to sleep. Most Hindu worship involves ARTI, a ceremony where a tray containing small lighted ghee candles is swung to a specific hymn in front of the deity. (*See also* DARSHAN; MANDIR)

Pujari Sometimes used to describe a village BRAHMIN priest but more accurately used as the title for a brahmin who conducts the worship at a temple or shrine and is mainly concerned with performance of ritual. (*See also* PANDIT, PUROHIT)

Punya An action that brings merit either in this life or the next. Although contemporary Hindus are beginning to use the term to mean right or moral actions, it was not originally understood in the context of morality. Merit and demerit were brought about by faulty or incorrect performance of ritual. This was then extended to include the incorrect performance of caste duties or failure to observe DHARMA. (*See also* PAP)

Puranas A series of scriptures which are part of the SMRITI collection. They are epic poems and stories which chronicle the sagas of various gods and tell the myths of creation. They contain many of Hinduism's best-known religious stories and many of the correct forms of worship for different deities. Traditionally, there are eighteen, six each for SHIVA, VISHNU and BRAHMA. The *Puranas* are first mentioned in the *Arthava Veda* but the majority was written in the first millennium CE and was the product of the development of theistic traditions in that period. (*See also* MAHAPURANAS)

Puri   The city in Orissa where the famous worship of JAGANNATHA, a form of KRISHNA, takes place.

Purohit   A BRAHMIN who functions as a family priest. He might conduct rituals and ceremonies for a number of families. (*See also* PANDIT; PUJARI)

Purusha   The term *purusha* is used in the RIG VEDA for the primordial man or cosmic being whose sacrifice brings the world into existence. In SAMKHYA philosophy it is one of the two eternal components of all existence. PRAKRITI is changeable nature and *purusha* is the unchangeable spirit. There is a difference in opinion as to whether the *purusha* is singular or plural. Some sects argue that there are many *purushas* and the way to liberation is to free the *purusha* from *prakriti* by the intellectual grasp of the true nature of *prakriti* and the denial of sense perception. Jain doctrines of liberation are very similar to the Samkhya philosophy. Once the *purusha* is liberated it exists in perfect and eternal isolation. For those who believe in one universal *purusha*, the goal remains to free oneself of *prakriti*. (*See also* PRAJAPATI)

Purva Mimansa   *See* MIMANSA.

Pushkar   A small pilgrimage town in Rajasthan sacred to BRAHMA. Although containing many temples surrounding a small lake, Pushkar is famous as it contains one of only two Brahma temples in India. The lake is holy, as it is believed to have been the place where Brahma and SARASWATI manifested on a lotus flower.

Pushti Marga   A large devotional sect founded by VALLABHA (1481–1533). It has several million followers in Northern India and many places of worship. Pushti Marga places great emphasis on the grace of God which cannot be deserved or won even though the devotee is committed to a spiritual life. Surrender of possessions and self to the GURU are essential for salvation, and service performed through pure and selfless love is emphasized. The way is open to all, including women and low-caste Hindus, but family life is extolled over and above renunciation. Pushti Marga, in common with other BHAKTI (devotional) movements, emphasizes the eternal enjoyment of God rather than MOKSHA (liberation) as the supreme goal of life. The GOPIS, the beloved companions of KRISHNA, are seen as the ideal of devotion. (*See also* SANT)

R

Radha The consort of KRISHNA first mentioned in the *Vishnu Purana* and *Bhagavada Purana*. The *Vishnu Purana* contains the stories of Krishna's exile amongst the cowherds of VRINDAVAN known as the GOPIS. The *Bhagavad Purana* develops these tales and introduces Radha as Krishna's favourite *gopi* and eventual consort. Many of mediaeval India's poets took up the theme of the love between Krishna and Radha as a great symbol of BHAKTI, or divine love. Radha came to be perceived as the ideal devotee and as an incarnation of the benign form of the Goddess SRI or LAKSHMI, the eternal consort of Vishnu. In the fifteenth century, CAITANYA, a Bengali BRAHMIN, ecstatic with the love of the Divine, created a form of Krishna worship based on dance and devotional music. He often impersonated Radha in order to identify with her perfect love for Krishna. There are some VAISHNAVITE movements that believe Caitanya to be the incarnation of both Radha and Krishna. (*See also* VAISHNAVISM)

Radhakrishnan (1888–1975) President of India from 1962–67 and one of the most influential figures in the renaissance of Hinduism that took place in the nineteenth and twentieth centuries. Radhakrishnan was not a renunciate or a creator of a new Hindu movement but an academic professor of philosophy. He had been deeply influenced by VIVEKANANDA and his attempts to portray Hinduism as a creditable and reasonable intellectual tradition based on the ideas of VEDANTA philosophy. Radhakrishnan became the foremost apologist for Hinduism and developed a rational view of his own tradition based on his understandings of Vedanta and the influence of Western rationalism and science.

Radhasoamis   A contemporary movement that has its roots in mid-nineteenth century Agra with the teachings of Shiv Dayal Singh. The movement can be considered as a modern form of the North Indian SANT tradition, influenced by the NIRGUNA BHAKTI (devotion to the formless God) of KABIR and the early Sikh Gurus, especially Nanak. However, in common with other contemporary Hindu movements it borrows from the universalism of figures such as RAMAKRISHNA and the eclecticism inherent within popular Hinduism. After Shiv Dayal Singh's death, the movement splintered into at least twenty organizations. The most successful flourished in the Punjab under the leadership of a succession of masters from Sikh background who claim direct descent from Shiv Dayal Singh. Their headquarters is a large ASHRAM on the banks of the River Beas, known as Satsang Beas. The Radhasoami movement has prospered in India and has major branches consisting of ashrams and hospitals throughout the country. Satsang Beas has attracted followers from outside the Hindu community, especially among Sikhs and Western spiritual seekers. (*See also* SANT MAT)

Raja Yoga   The royal or supreme YOGA described as the path of self-control performed to comprehend reality or the Self through direct experience. Although spoken about by KRISHNA in the BHAGAVAD GITA, *Raja Yoga* was fully defined as a system by PATANJALI in the YOGA SUTRAS. He describes yoga as the 'cessation of all changes of consciousness' and outlines an eightfold path that constitutes a fully developed meditation discipline. The stages of the path are abstention or self-control, observance of the rules of devotion, posture, breath control, sense control, fixed concentration, and complete onepointedness. (*See also* ASANA; DHARANA; DHYANA; NIYAMA; PRANAYAMA; PRATYAHARA; SAMADHI; YAMA)

Rajas   One of the three GUNAS or qualities that mix in varying proportions to form all created beings and material entities. *Rajas* denotes the quality of energy or activity sometimes translated as passion. In inanimate objects, rajas would provide energy or movement. It would be more manifest in the energetic forces of nature such as wind or fire. In the human being *rajas* manifests as a passionate nature and is the source of emotions such as anger, hatred, ambition, pride and sexual desire. Some VAISHNAVITE traditions have classified foods according to the predominate *guna*. Some foods such as onions and garlic, for example, are believed to create sexual passion and anger. However, *rajas* can be a positive force when restrained by DHARMA and can be utilized for the service of society in the warrior caste, for example (KSHRATIYA). However, *rajas* is considered an obstacle to spiritual enlightenment, and its influence on human nature would need to be overcome to secure liberation (MOKSHA) or final release from SAMSARA. (*See also* PRAKRITI; RAJASIK; SATTVA; TAMAS; VAISNAVISM)

Rajasik Either someone whose nature is dominated by RAJAS, the GUNA that promotes anger and lust, or the typology of food that promotes those qualities in a human being.

Rakhi An amulet made of silk or cotton thread which is placed on the wrist to give protection and increase the bond of mutual love. It is tied by a groom on the left wrist of the bride at Hindu weddings. (*See also* RAKSHA BANDHAN)

Raksha Manifestations of supernatural beings that live in celestial or demonic realms. They possess powers that would be considered miraculous to human beings but they are not divine. They are part of the world of SAMSARA and will be subject to death and rebirth even though their life spans are very long.

Raksha Bandhan The festival in which women tie RAKHIS onto their brothers' wrists in order to express the bond of love and demonstrate their appreciation for the protection a brother offers.

Ram Mohan Roy (1772–1833) Born in Bengal, Ram Mohan Roy was originally influenced by Muslim monotheism and the monistic interpretation of the UPANISHADS taught by ADVAITA VEDANTA. He studied English and went on to develop a strong interest in European philosophy and religious ideas. He accepted the common critique of Hinduism current amongst the British in India – that Hinduism was a degenerate version of a once great philosophical tradition. He wanted to reform Hinduism in the light of European Christian thought and knowledge and embarked on a campaign to restore the Vedic tradition as the original form of Hindu monotheism. In response to Christian missionary criticism of Hinduism as a polytheistic idol-worshipping religion steeped in superstitious practices, he founded the BRAHMO SAMAJ, first known as the British India Unitarian Association, to propagate a Hinduism based on the philosophical ideas of the *Upanishads*. The movement is one of the first of those reform movements that are sometimes called neo-Hinduism and was the forerunner of contemporary Hindu ideas based on rational interpretation of VEDANTA. (*See also* DAYANANDA; RADHAKRISHNAN; VIVEKANANDA)

Rama Along with KRISHNA, one of the two most commonly worshipped AVATARS of VISHNU, especially popular in North India. Rama is the hero of the RAMAYANA and believed to be the manifestation of DHARMA. He was born as the son of King DASARATHA, an aged ruler of the Kingdom of Kosala. The king had performed sacrifices in order to produce sons. Vishnu agreed to manifest partially in all the three offspring of the king by his three wives but to incarnate completely as Rama, the fourth son. The story of Rama is told in several versions of the great epic, the *Ramayana*, but the two most famous are the original Sanskrit version attributed to VALMIKI and the later mediaeval version by TULSIDAS, correctly known as the RAMACHARITAMANASA. (*See also* SITA)

Ramacharitamanasa A Hindi version of the RAMAYANA, written by the sixteenth-century BHAKTI poet and saint TULSIDAS, that was able to reach the common people in a way that the Sanskrit version by VALMIKI could not achieve. Tulsidas wrote the work in VARANASI in the late sixteenth century. The storyline is basically the same as Valmiki's version but the major difference is the emphasis on devotion that is apparent throughout the text. Although the book acknowledges the orthodox BRAHMIN tradition asserted in the *Ramayana*, it introduces the universal possibility of salvation to women, outcastes and low-castes. This is achieved by remembrance of God's true name. In this respect, the work is highly influenced by the *bhakti* and SANT traditions that were so popular in mediaeval North India. Tulsidas's version of the epic is extremely popular throughout Northern India and has influenced religious life immensely. The famous RAMLILA performances are all based on the *Ramacharitamanasa* and the text is recited throughout Hindi-speaking North India.

Ramakrishna   (1836–86). A Hindu mystic often associated with nineteenth-century reform and revival of Hinduism. He was born in a small village in Bengal but followed his brother to Calcutta where he eventually became the priest at the KALI temple at Dakshineshwar near Calcutta. Although he began as a devotee of the Goddess, during his life he achieved an extraordinary range of personal experiences of the divine. Throughout his life he practiced intense meditation and prayer and experienced visions and unitative states of God-awareness. He followed a variety of Hindu paths or SADHANAS under the guidance of various teachers who visited Dakshineshwar. He practiced TANTRA, VEDANTA and VAISHNAVITE traditions of deep devotion to an ISHWARA (personal form) of VISHNU. He also looked at Muslim and Christian teachings and received visions of Muhammad and Jesus. His deep experiences on all these paths prompted him to teach that all the main religions can lead to God. He began to attract a group of disciples including students from the undergraduates in Calcutta University. After his death many of them formed a renunciate order and began the RAMAKRISHNA MISSION. His most famous disciple, Swami VIVEKANANDA, took the message out of India to North America and Europe. The significance of Ramakrishna in the development of contemporary Hinduism cannot be underestimated. He united the traditional Hinduism, especially that of the ecstatic saint figure drunk on the love of God, to the new rational forms of Hinduism that were developing in India under the influence of Western rationalism and Christianity. The idea that all religions lead to God because they are all variations of the SANATAN DHARMA (eternal truth) is now endemic amongst Hindus. Ramakrishna is regarded by millions of Hindus as a contemporary incarnation of the Divine. (*See also* VAISHNAVISM).

Ramakrishna Mission   When RAMAKRISHNA died in 1886, he had not founded a sect or society or even written a book, but his closest followers were dedicated in promoting his teachings throughout India and the world. In order to achieve this aim the Ramakrishna Mission was founded by VIVEKANANDA, a close disciple of the saint. Today there are branches of the Ramakrishna Mission throughout India with its headquarters in Calcutta. Typically a centre or ASHRAM of the mission will include a library, hostel, hospital and prayer or meditation hall. Usually, the meditation hall will contain murals of all the great figures of the world's religions in accord with Ramakrishna's teachings that all religions are pathways to God. The central focus of worship is a statue of the saint himself, surrounded by the normal paraphernalia of Hindu temple worship. Vivekananda established several branches of the Ramakrishna Mission in the West, but they are often registered as the Vedanta Society. His missionary activity in the Western world was the forerunner for the explosion of interest in oriental philosophy and spiritual practices in the 1960s and 1970s.

Ramana Maharshi   (1879–1950) Another of the significant modern Hindu mystics who contributed to the development of contemporary Hinduism and the promotion of ADVAITA teachings in the West. Ramana Maharshi was born in South India and at the age of seventeen underwent a deep experience in which his sense of body consciousness dissolved to leave him with an intuitive feeling of identification with the inner eternal spirit. The impact of this experience never left him and shortly after he took up residence as a renunciate on the local pilgrimage site at Arunachala. He was deeply influenced by ADVAITA VEDANTA and taught by consistently asking visitors to the sacred mountain to deeply consider the question 'who are you?' He eventually attracted thousands of visitors, many of whom became disciples. He was visited by Paul Brunton, the orientalist, who went on to write many books on Hindu spirituality and helped to prepare the soil for the explosion of interest in Eastern spirituality in the West during the 1960s and 1970s.

Ramananda   A fourteenth century VAISHNAVITE who is believed to have been a direct spiritual descendent of RAMANUJA. Ramananda worshipped God in the form of the VISHNU AVATAR, RAMA. In common with many of the North Indian mediaeval BHAKTI (devotion) figures, he allowed everyone, including women and low-caste members, to become his followers. His most famous disciple is believed to have been KABIR. Today, the Ramananada movement is one of the biggest SAMPRA-DAYAS (sects) in Northern India. It is known as the *Sri Sampradaya* with its headquarters in AYODHYA, the pilgrimage city associated with Rama. The followers, known as Ramanandis, worship Rama and SITA at several hundred centres throughout India. They are mostly poor uneducated people known for the fervour of their devotion. They tattoo the name of Rama on their skin and adopt the suffix of '*dasa*' (servant or slave) to their names. (*See also* VAISHNAVISM)

Ramanuja (d. 1137) A Hindu philosopher and BRAHMIN who opposed the ADVAITA VEDANTA philosophy of SHANKARA. He objected to Shankara's basic premise that BRAHMAN and ATMAN are identical. He posited the view that the God and devotee were separate in order that the central relationship of loving worship could take place. He was a great devotee of VISHNU and maintained that God, souls and the world are all real, but that the last two depend completely on God. The created universe is regarded as the body of God rather than illusion (MAYA). Ramanuja wrote extensive commentaries on VEDANTA SUTRA, UPANISHADS and the BHAGAVAD GITA. His interpretation of the *Bhagavad* emphasizes monotheism and personal devotion rather than Shankara's monism. Consequently Ramanuja can be considered the philosopher *par excellence* of the *bhakti* (devotional) tradition, although, unlike the later *bhakti* movement of mediaeval Hinduism, he did not advocate universalism. Ramanuja's school of Vedanta is known as VISHISHTAD-VAITA or Qualified Non-Dualism. After his death, his followers divided into main schools known as the cat (*marjara*) and monkey (*markata*). The former developed in South India and taught that the devotee was completely dependent on God's grace for spiritual development as the kitten is carried by the mother-cat. The latter developed in North India and advocated that the devotee developed by spiritual effort as the infant monkey clings on to the mother when she travels. (*See also* VAISHNAVISM)

Ramayana The Sanskrit version of the great epic which recounts the saga of RAMA and SITA. It is attributed to the sage VALMIKI and was written somewhere between 400–300 BCE. Although the *Ramayana* is essentially VAISHNAVITE (worship of VISHNU) in its doctrine it contains strong elements of the Shaivite (worship of SHIVA) tradition and represents the move towards eclecticism so dominant in modern Hinduism. The *Ramayana* consists of seven books (*kandas*), although some scholars have argued that the first and last are later additions to the narrative. It recounts the adventures of Rama, the incarnation of Vishnu, from his birth to his exile from his father's kingdom. It goes on to explore his wandering in the jungle with his wife, Sita and brother, LAKSHMAN, where Rama rescues BRAHMINS and sages from their persecution by demons. Sita is kidnapped by the demon-king, RAVANA, and the Ramayana goes on to recount Rama's search for his wife, the war with Ravana and the eventual triumphant return to AYODHYA. Rama is considered to be the AVATAR (incarnation) of Vishnu and is the personification of DHARMA. Consequently, the original *Ramayana* represents orthodox Brahminical tradition but later versions such as the RAMACHARITAMANASA incorporate the more revolutionary teachings of the BHAKTI (devotional) tradition that subverts Brahmin hegemony of the religious teachings of Hinduism. (*See also* HANUMAN; SHAIVISM; TULSIDAS; VAISHNAVISM)

Ramlila A popular festival in North India that incorporates DASSERA, replacing NAVARATRI, and celebrates the victory of RAMA over RAVANA, the demon-king of Sri Lanka. The festival usually lasts for several days during which Rama's story, as recounted in the RAMAYANA, is acted out. The festival ends with the burning of effigies of Ravana combined with large firework displays. The most elaborate form of *Ramlila* takes place in VARANASI and lasts for one month. The Maharaja of Varanasi still traditionally attends the complete festival and at the culmination of Rama's triumphant return, the whole town of Ramnagar, near Varanasi, is turned into AYODHYA. (*See also* RAMACHARITAMANASA)

Ramnavami / Ramnavmi The birthday celebration of RAMA more popularly celebrated in North India where the worship of Rama is very strong. (*See also* RAMAYANA; RAMLILA)

Rasa A scale of devotional feeling developed in GAUDIYA VAISHNAVISM, an intensely emotional form of KRISHNA worship. Traditionally there are nine *rasas* that can be experienced by the devotee. The idea is to subsume a variety of human emotions into one-pointed devotion to Krishna as the object of all human feeling. The emotions that are transformed are: erotic love, laughter, compassion and pain, anger, frustration, fear, admiration and tranquility.

Rasalila The dance performed by the GOPIS, the cowherd devotees of KRISHNA, in the forests of VRINDAVAN. It is said that each *gopi* longed to dance with Krishna personally. He obliged by manifesting in a separate form for each one. The Rasalila is performed by Hindu dancers in various parts of India. (*See also* RADHA)

Ravana The many-headed demon-king of Sri Lanka who kidnapped SITA, the faithful wife of RAMA, the human AVATAR of VISHNU. A large part of the saga of Rama is taken up with his search for Sita and the eventual war with RAVANA. Ravana is extremely powerful due to austerities practised in a previous life and almost defeats Rama and his allies. It is believed by some devotional movements that Ravana was, in fact, a great devotee as he was obsessed with Rama. This corresponds with the devotee's aim to never forget the name of the Lord. Rama's triumph over Ravana can also be seen symbolically as the triumph of the soul over evil. The many-headed Ravana can be viewed as the endless desires of the human mind that have to be overcome before liberation or salvation can be achieved. (*See also* RAMAYANA)

Ravidas A well-known North-Indian mystic of the SANT tradition who belonged to the *chamar* (cobbler) caste. He was born in the Hindu city of VARANASI, where he attracted many followers through his teachings promoting love of God and self-surrender. Like Guru Nanak and KABIR he extolled *nam simaran* as the only practice able to liberate human beings. Sikhs acknowledge the life and teachings of Ravidas by including his poems in the Guru Granth Sahib. Today, many Hindu and Sikh *chamars* belong to the Ravidasis, the followers of Ravidas. Their temples are known as *gurdwaras* where they also install the

Guru Granth Sahib. Many of their practices are indistinguishable from Sikh religious practices.

Rig Veda   The major SHRUTI text and to orthodox Hindus the most sacred and ancient of the Hindu scriptures. It was probably composed around 1500 BCE but Hindus believe its Sanskrit hymns and sacred formulas to be eternal and revealed to ancient RISHIS (sages) in their meditation. Although there are many strands to the *Rig Veda*, its central theme is the sacrificial fire ceremony performed by the BRAHMINS to maintain cosmic order (RTA). The *Rig Veda* sees the original sacrifice performed by the gods as the primal cause of creation. The text is still essentially the preserve of the brahmin caste who uses its sacred formulas for their rituals, ceremonies and Hindu rites of passage. It is studied and interpreted in the MIMANSA school of orthodox philosophy so that the brahmins are versed in the correct performance of ritual. (*See also* VEDAS)

Rishi   The ancient seers or sages of the ARYAN civilization who are believed to have received the original revelation of the Vedas in their meditation. They are still traditionally propitiated by the BRAHMIN priests. (*See also* VEDAS)

Rta / Ritam   The Vedic concept of the cosmic law – guarded by the two gods, VARUNA and MITRA – that maintains all existence. Human order (DHARMA) was also considered to be part of *rta* and consequently anyone who broke the ordinances of society was guilty of violating the cosmic order. From this concept developed the law of *dharma* and KARMA. Although *dharma* is now associated with moral law, the central concern of the VEDAS was the maintenance of cosmic order through the correct performance of sacrificial ritual. The intricate codes of moral law associated with caste observances developed later and were formulated in the LAWS OF MANU.

Rudra   A minor deity of the RIG VEDA who is the father of the Maruts, the storm gods. Rudra was feared for his destructive powers and control over the forces of nature. Consequently, he was held in awe and was given the titles '*siva*' (auspicious), '*samkara*' (beneficent), and '*sambhu*' (benign) in the YAJUR VEDA. In other ancient texts, he is called '*Hara*' (the destroyer). He was believed to bestow healing and offer protection against the forces of nature. By the time that the SVETASVATARA UPANISHAD had been written, Rudra was identified with BRAHMAN in a more personal form. The *Upanishad* is essentially theistic and advocates the path of salvation through devotion to the personal God identified as Rudra or SHIVA. Thus the ancient storm deity of the VEDAS developed into Shiva, the personal manifestation of Brahman, the supreme spirit and ruler of the world and the human self and probably the most popularly worshipped deity in Hinduism. (*See also* SHAIVISM)

S

Sabda Brahman The supreme being, the formless BRAHMAN, in the form of sound. This primeval uncreated sound is believed to be the medium between the formless Brahman and the material world. Some YOGIS and practitioners of spiritual paths claim to be able to hear this sound in their meditations. The idea of an unstruck sound has given rise to the important concept of MANTRA meditation in Hindu religious traditions. (*See also* OM)

Sadhana / Sadhan The spiritual practice or discipline followed by an adherent of a particular path believed to lead to liberation or salvation. A GURU usually teaches it to his disciple through an initiation. (*See also* DIKSHA)

Sadhu / Saddhu A wandering holy man or woman who has renounced the life of a householder. They may be part of a sectarian movement or an independent practitioner but their lifestyle should embrace celibacy, homelessness, SADHANA and minimum possessions. They will gather at pilgrimage places in their distinctive saffron robes, often with long matted hair or shaved heads. The sectarian orders of *sadhus* generally maintain ASHRAMS where they can stay and practice their spiritual disciplines or preach to lay members and visitors. The practices of *sadhus* reflect the breadth and depth of Hinduism but some are known for their ascetic lifestyles and practice of austerities. (*See also* SANNYASIN)

Saguna *Lit. with form or qualities.* Used to describe the qualities or aspects of the divine. Hindu philosophy has been divided over the question whether the Absolute Reality has qualities or form. It can be argued that most of the early schools of philosophy were non-theistic and therefore did not see the Absolute as having qualities but later theistic movements merged the pantheon of deities into a henotheistic umbrella where each individual worshipper chose his or her own deity as a manifestation of the Supreme Being. This personal theism resulted in the Impersonal Absolute acquiring a host of personal qualities and manifestations. (*See also* ISHWARA; NIRGUNA BRAHMAN; SAGUNA BRAHMAN)

Saguna bhakti   Devotion to one of the forms of the divine acknowledged in Hinduism, or alternatively worship of a living or deceased GURU as a manifestation of the divine. (*See also* BHAKTI; ISHWARA; SAGUNA; SAGUNA BRAHMAN)

Saguna Brahman / Sagunam Brahman   Brahman or the Supreme Being endowed with form or qualities and becoming the personal God or ISHWARA. It is usually acknowledged that Brahman contains the qualities of SAT (truth), CHIT (consciousness) and ANAND (bliss) but is otherwise impersonal. The dedicated adherent of certain practices may find Brahman as their own innermost reality (ATMAN) but most BHAKTI-orientated movements go further and apply to Brahman attributes such as love, grace and compassion. The term SAGUNA is also used to describe the incarnations of the supreme being (AVATARS) into animal or human form in order to perform a saving act. The images of these *avatars* maintained in temples are believed to be enlivened by the presence of the actual deity. Thus a devotee who focuses on a MURTI or temple deity may also believe that he/she worships God with form and attributes. There are arguments between various Hindu movements over whether the form or the formless appears first as the ultimate reality. Many VAISHNAVITE movements argue that their chosen VISHNU *ishwara* pre-exists the formless God who is perceived to be an infinite emanation of the radiant form of God. (*See also* NIRGUNA BRAHMAN; SATCHITANAND; VAISHNAVISM; VEDANTA)

Sahasrara   The ultimate CHAKRA (power centre) situated at the top of the inside of the skull and generally symbolized in Hindu sacred art as the thousand-petalled lotus. The YOGI performs various practices designed to raise the female KUNDALINI energy located at the base of the spine which then travels up through the SUSUMNA psychic canal through the various *chakras* until it unites in SAMADHI with the SHIVA energy stored in the SAHASRAHA. (*See also* TANTRA)

Sakti *See* SHAKTI.

Salagram *See* SHALAGRAM.

Sama Veda The VEDA that arranges the verses of the RIG VEDA into a form that can be chanted in ritual worship by the *udgatar* (the priest who chants at the Vedic sacrifice). (*See also* YAJNA)

Samadhi The condition of one-pointed focus on the object of meditation to the degree that subject-object consciousness is completely lost thus resulting in a state of awareness that experiences complete oneness. In Tantric yoga, *samadhi* results from the union of the KUNDALINI with the SAHASRAHA, but SADHANAS (spiritual disciplines) may teach MANTRA meditation or breath techniques. In theistic traditions of Hinduism, *samadhi* is understood to be complete absorption into the experience of the Divine usually discovered within. In this state all sense of individual self and ego are lost. Whatever the difference in regard to theistic or non-theistic traditions, *samadhi* is perceived to be, above all, the state of unitive consciousness. It is generally believed that the person who achieves *samadhi* is liberated from bondage to the cycle of birth and death, although some sects believe that final release may only be achieved after death. (*See also* TANTRA; YOGA)

Samdhya The morning prayer observed by millions of practising Hindus that takes place from just before sunrise and ends when the sun's disk is fully above the horizon. The main prayer is the GAYATRI MANTRA repeated several times, but various sects have their own versions and some BRAHMIN priests use a longer form of the prayer that contains verses from the PURANAS and a ritual to drive away evil.

Samkhya / Sankhya   One of the six orthodox schools of philosophy, possibly founded in the seventh century BCE, though its teachings are found in the *Samkhya Karika*, attributed to Isvarakrishna, probably written at a later date somewhere between the second to fourth centuries BCE. Samkhya philosophy is essentially non-theistic and views the cosmos as made up of two eternally existing energies known as PURUSHA and PRAKRITI. *Prakriti* consists of twenty-four kinds of energy and matter that include mental experiences in a state of constant flux. The twenty-fifth category is *purusha*, the individual but eternal changeless spirit. The aim of Samkhya is to bring about self-identification with the *purusha* and release it from the bondage of *prakriti*. The *purusha* then lives in eternal but blissful self-being. The YOGA school, however, only accepts a supreme *purusha*, or ISHWARA, in the capacity of assisting the practitioner as the focus for meditation rather than an object of worship. (*See also* DARSHANA)

Samkirtana   *See* KIRTAN.

Samnyasin   *See* SANNYASIN.

Sampradaya   The correct term for the countless sects that exist within the framework of Hinduism. Although the three foremost divisions of Hindu belief and practice are VAISHNIVISM (Vishnu worship), SHAIVISM (Shiva worship) and SHAKTI (Goddess worship), these are not sects as each one contains many sects within the tradition. Hindu sects are usually the result of individual spiritual teachers (GURUS) and are developed historically after the founder's death. They will each contain a distinct set of beliefs and practices but maintain the central themes of SAMSARA (cycle of birth and death), KARMA (law of action and reaction) and MUKTI (liberation). Hindu sects are rarely exclusive and followers may well belong to other forms of Hindu practice. Sects continue to develop, as Hinduism remains a living tradition that produces many holy men and women.

Samsara / Sansara   It is a central belief in all Indian traditions that all beings are caught in an endless ocean of continuous rebirths or a continuous and eternal process of coming and going from one life to another which only ceases when the soul achieves liberation or MUKTI. *Samsara* refers not only to the process of endless birth and death, but also to the worlds where rebirth is possible. This includes the worlds of animals, humans, demons, gods and demi-gods. Rebirth can take place in any of the countless forms that inhabit these realms. The inner world of the mind is also included in *samsara* as it is created or formed. In general *samsara* is everything that is created, survives for a duration and then decays or dies; it is the process of endless change as opposed to BRAHMAN or ATMAN, the changeless reality that lies behind and within *samsara*. (*See also* KARMA)

Samskar / Samskara / Sanskar   Rites of passage or life-cycle rituals that mark a new stage in life. There are a total of sixteen that begin before birth with conception and continue after death, but not all Hindus observe them all. The most important are birth, naming, first haircut, receiving the sacred thread, betrothal and marriage, taking vows of renunciation, death and rites for the dead. The rules for the performance of *samskaras* are contained in the *Grihya Sutras*, written in the last few centuries BCE. (*See also* SHRADDHA; UPANAYANA)

Samyasin   *See* SANNYASIN.

Sanatan Dharma   *Lit. the eternal religion.* Many Hindus prefer the Sanskrit term '*sanatan* DHARMA' to describe their religious practice and belief. It is believed that the original form of Hinduism was revealed in the VEDAS to RISHIS or sages. However, as Hindus believe in an endless cycle of creation and destruction, the *Vedas* are given again to human beings at the beginning of each cycle of creation. Other Hindus use the term to describe the end goal, of oneness with BRAHMAN, the absolute reality, as the eternal quest of all living beings.

Sangha   An assembly of sages or holy men and women who have come together to worship God. In BHAKTI (devotional) movements, the Sangha would usually come together to hear discourses praising God or to take part in congregational singing. (*See also* KIRTAN; SATSANG)

Sankhya   *See* SAMKHYA.

Sannyasin / Samyasin / Samnyasin / Sennyasin   A man or woman who has completely cut all ties with the world and renounced worldly affairs. In classical Hinduism this is regarded as the fourth and final stage of life that should be entered by individuals that are born into the twice-born VARNAS. It is, however, possible, to become a *sannyasin* at any stage of one's life and take up the life of a wandering monk. *Sannyasins* can belong to large orders founded by particular individuals or they can be solitary wanderers. They are expected to follow some kind of SADHANA (spiritual discipline) that will allow them to focus only on the goal of liberation. The *sannyasin* is the only individual who is regarded to be outside of caste and its duties. (*See also* MUKTI; SADHU)

Sanskrit   The classical language of the ARYANS used to write many of the ancient Hindu and Buddhist scriptures. It is still used in ritual worship and studied by the BRAHMIN priests.

Sant   The term used to collectively describe the North-Indian devotional movements which date from the mediaeval period. The *sants* criticized the outward forms of religion and emphasized the inner experience and the guidance of the SATGURU. Sikhism acknowledges their teachings by including the poems of several prominent *sants* in the *Guru Granth Sahib*. The term is also used to describe a Sikh spiritual leader with a personal following. In this way, the problem of using the contro-versial term GURU can be avoided. The followers of Sikh *sants* display all the behaviour towards them of discipleship but the *sants* themselves acknowledge the authority of the *Guru Granth Sahib*.

Sant Mat   *Lit. the path of the sants.* Increasingly since the mediaeval period, India has produced holy men and women who, in vernacular languages and often using song and poetry, have preached a message that God is to be found within the heart of the devotee. The SANTS were opposed to caste distinction, gender inequality and even religious differences on the grounds of their conviction that God was the inner reality of all. They were also iconoclasts and often criticized the exoteric emphasis of both Hinduism and Islam. Some go as far as to state that all the outer phenomena of religion – rituals, ceremonies, austerities, fasting, pilgrimage, etc. – are of no consequence in achieving direct experiential knowledge of God. The *sants* promoted a threefold path that lead to experiential devotion: SATGURU, SATSANG and SATNAM. The first was the necessity of meeting a true GURU who could show one the way to experience the Divine within. The second encouraged the followers of the path to meet and share in their experiences through song and preaching; the last advocated the constant remembrance of the true Name of God as the only spiritual practice to bear fruit in the Age of Darkness. Famous *sants* are KABIR, NAMDEV, SURDAS, Lalla, TULSIDAS and the Sikh Gurus. (*See also* NIRGUNA BHAKTI)

Saraswati   The consort of BRAHMA and the Goddess of learning, the arts and the power of knowledge. In temples, her MURTI (image) is depicted as a white-skinned woman with two arms; one is holding a stringed instrument known as the *veena*. She rides upon a peacock.

Sat   *Lit. truth.* One of the three attributes or qualities of BRAHMAN according to VEDANTA. It refers to changelessness or existence. The UPANISHADS explained that behind the changing phenomena of the universe was an unchanging reality that gave existence out of itself to all individual beings. This eternal Being was *sat* because when everything would pass away, the existence of Brahman would remain, thus it was Truth, the Real. (*See also* ANAND; ATMAN; CHIT; SATCHITANANDA)

Satchitananda   In Vedantic philosophy, the name that describes all three essential attributes of BRAHMAN, the supreme Being, namely truth (SAT), consciousness (CHIT) and joy (ANAND). The ATMAN (the individual soul) also shares in the nature of Brahman and therefore has the same three qualities, just as a spark has the same qualities as the fire, or a drop of water has the same qualities as the ocean. (*See also* VEDANTA)

Satguru   *Lit. the true teacher.* Used in SANT traditions and other SAMPRADAYAS either as a name for God or to describe the perfect human GURU. It generally refers to a holy man who has the commission from God, or the teacher before him, to reveal the inner path which leads to discovery of God dwelling within the human being. The term is commonly used in the poetry of the Sikh Gurus and other North Indian *sants*. (*See also* SATNAM)

Sati / Suttee   The outlawed practice of widows immolating themselves on the funeral pyres of their dead husbands. There are countless village shrines belonging to those who successfully followed their husbands into death.

Satkaryavada   A theory of KARMA, the law of cause and effect, held by the SAMKHYA school of philosophy that states that the effect will always be identical to the cause. This idea is generally believed by the majority of Hindus.

Satnam   Often used by the SANT traditions as synonymous with God. It refers to the true Name of God which is revealed by the SATGURU to his followers. SAT refers to that which is constant or unchangeable. The *sant* teachers all spoke of a Name of God which pre-existed creation and which could be discovered by seekers of truth within themselves. The tongue or the mind does not repeat it but it is self-repeated in the inner rhythm of life.

Satsang   *Lit. company of truth*. A term commonly used by the SANTS and the followers of the BHAKTI tradition. TULSIDAS describes *Satsang* as a genuine enthusiasm to listen to the praises of God but the term has entered the common parlance of Hinduism and can be used to describe either the gathering of devotees to partake in KIRTAN (communal devotional singing) or the discourse of a GURU to disciples or any kind of religious public gathering.

Sattva / Sattwa   According to SAMKHYA philosophy, *sattva* is one of the three GUNAS or qualities of nature that, in infinite variations, form PRAKRITI or primordial matter. *Sattva* is the quality of harmony, balance or goodness; sometimes it is translated as brightness. A wise person tries to cultivate the quality of *sattva* through harmonious living, peacefulness, meditation and a vegetarian diet consisting of fresh fruit, vegetables and dairy products. The qualities that arise from a more *sattvic* nature will not in themselves lead to closer proximity to

BRAHMAN or PURUSHA (the Absolute reality) but will lead to the increased desire for Knowledge of Brahman and a life of devotion. (*See also* RAJAS; TAMAS)

Satyagraha *Lit. soul-force or truth-force.* MAHATMA GANDHI's philosophy of non-violent action used so successfully against the British in the independence movement. Gandhi insisted that India would first have to conquer herself through self-restraint and a return to the moral values of the Hindu scriptures and sages before it would be possible to remove the British. He set out to establish the example that the rest of India should follow. The independence movement therefore had a moral and religious dimension to its political ambitions.

Sat Yuga *See* KRTA YUGA.

Savitri A woman who represents the ideal of motherhood. Her story is recorded in the MAHABHARATA. She was the daughter of a barren king who had prayed for a child to the Goddess of the same name. She grew up to be so virtuous and beautiful that all men were intimidated by her and she could not find a husband. Eventually, she fell in love with Satyavit, the son of a blind king, who had been brought up in a forest hermitage. However, Satyavit only had a year to live. At the time of his impending death, Savitri fasted and performed penance. When YAMA, the god of death, came to escort Satyavit's soul from its body, Savitri followed the god and would not leave. He offered her many boons but she could not ask for her husband to return to life. She succeeded in obtaining her father's sight and his lost kingdom. Eventually she tricked Yama by asking for sons for herself. When the god agreed, she managed to persuade him to release her husband or, otherwise, she would lose her virtue. Savitri is regarded as the ideal wife and daughter and the model of resolution.

Sennyasin *See* SANNYASIN.

Sesa *Lit. remainder.* The thousand-headed snake also known as *Ananta* (endless) upon which VISHNU, the cosmic preserver, sleeps and observes the cycles of successive creation and destruction.

Shaiva Agamas   A group of twenty-eight scriptures held to be sacred by the followers of SHAIVA SIDDHANTA. The first was probably written around the sixth century BCE. They teach the worship of the ultimate being in the form of SHIVA and the different ways to liberation in relation to Shiva as divine reality.

Shaiva Siddhanta   An ancient and still vigorous tradition of SHIVA worship that is strong in Tamil-speaking India. The followers of *Shaiva Siddhanta* regard Shiva as the ultimate reality, the origin and end of all things. The tradition acknowledges a sacred canon made up of the VEDAS, the UPANISHADS, the SHAIVA AGAMAS, twelve *tirumurai*, or books that contain devotional poetry, and fourteen Meykanta Sastras, mediaeval theological works. The theology of the tradition centres around three concepts: *Pati* (God in the form of Shiva, *Pashu* (the soul) and *Pasha* (fetters). The soul is kept in bondage by *pasha* and may only be released by the love of Shiva who is an immanent and transcendent personal God full of boundless bliss and intelligence. He is creator, preserver, destroyer and also personal saviour to his devotees. All other deities are under his control and he is immanent in creation as SHAKTI, his creative power, which is known as the Goddess. The practices of the tradition are various rituals, YOGA and personal discipline. At the highest level a GURU is required. In the state of final liberation, the soul remains individual but lives in state of pure bliss and devotion to Shiva. It is therefore possible to speak about salvation rather than liberation in this context.

Shaivism   The worship of SHIVA and his family, which alongside VAISH-NAVISM (worship of Vishnu and his forms) and the worship of the Goddess, forms one of the largest constituents of Hinduism. Generally speaking, the family of Shiva consists of PARVATI, his wife and consort, and their two sons, GANESH and KARTIKEYA. The Shaivite tradition comprises hundreds of sects of which some are made up of renunciates who regard Shiva as the ultimate ascetic. (*See also* SHAIVA SIDDHANTA; TANTRA)

Shakta   One who worships the Goddess in any one of her countless forms or, more specifically, someone who follows the path of TANTRA. (*See also* SHAKTI)

Shakta Agamas   A group of scriptures held to be sacred by the followers of TANTRA. They teach the worship of spiritual power in the form of the Divine Mother or Goddess. (*See also* SHAKTI)

Shakti / Sakti   The active energy or power of the divine that is manifest in creation. It is usually associated with the power of the Goddess as present in nature or with PRAKRITI, the primordial matter described in SAMKHYA philosophy. Sometimes she is identified with MAYA, the veiling power that hides BRAHMAN from the individual human soul. Shakti is also used to describe the path of devotion to the forms of the Goddess or universal Mother as opposed to VAISHNAVISM or SHAIVISM, the worship of VISHNU or SHIVA. There are a vast variety of forms of the Goddess. Many of them are consorts of major Hindu deities or AVATARS. Principal amongst these are SRI, LAKSHMI, SITA, RADHA, SARASWATI, DURGA and PARVATI. Other goddesses exist as independent from any male; the most important amongst these is KALI.

Shalagram / Salagram   A smooth tubular stone containing Ammonite fossil with spiral markings on the inside, particularly revered by the devotees of VISHNU. It is one of the symbols of Vishnu and the inner markings are believed to be representations of his discus. It is kept wrapped in a cloth and ritually bathed. The water is then drunk to remove sins and impurities. (*See also* VAISHNAVISM)

Shankara   (788–820 CE) A Hindu sage and philosopher famed for his development of ADVAITA VEDANTA in which he propounded the belief that ATMAN and BRAHMAN are identical. Born in Kerala in South India, he renounced the world to become a SANNYASIN at the age of eighteen. He is well-known for engaging his philosophical opponents in debate and Hindus believe that he was responsible for the decline in Indian Buddhism and the revival of Vedic Hinduism. This belief certainly exaggerates the role of Shankara but there is no doubt that he was a formidable philosopher and reformer. In his short life span he wrote several books and commentaries but also succeeded in organizing Hindu renunciates into four orders each established in Shankara's respective headquarters in the North, South, East and West of India. These four orders remain dominant amongst Hindu renunciates and the four centres are now led by hereditary leaders, known as Shankaracharyas, who are still major Hindu religious leaders.

Shanti The condition of inner peace that is felt in meditation, worship, or the presence of the Divine. It is also believed that *shanti* can be felt in sacred places or in the quietness of nature.

Shashthi The universal Mother or Goddess in the form of the protector of children, commonly worshipped by women in their homes. (*See also* SHAKTI)

Shikhara The traditional tower or spire built on top of the shrine room in a Hindu temple. (*See also* GARBHA-GRIHA; MANDIR)

Shitala Mata The Goddess of Smallpox or epidemic diseases. She is generally worshipped in the villages, although there is a famous temple in VARANASI. She is regarded as unmarried and full of hot anger. Her victims are cured by propitiating her through animal sacrifice and cooling rituals.

Shiva / Siva *Lit. the auspicious or gentle.* Sometimes regarded as part of the triad or triune God, BRAHMA, VISHNU and SHIVA. In this context he represents the destructive power in the constant process of change. He is also seen as the great YOGI and is regarded highly by many SADHUS. Many Hindus regard Shiva as the ultimate reality in himself, and his sects constitue the vast variety that make up the Shaivite tradition. The cult of Shiva is very ancient, and it is speculated that it goes back to the pre-ARYAN cultures of Northern India, particularly the Indus Valley civilizations. Although Shiva is unknown by name in the VEDAS, the storm-god, RUDRA, has many of his attributes. Shiva is first used in the UPANISHADS to describe the personal form of the impersonal BRAHMAN, the ultimate reality. The PURANAS describe Shiva in greater detail but represent many images of the God: from a fierce deity, associated with death and time, who wears skulls and snakes around his body and lives in cremation grounds, to the chaste renunciate who eventually marries PARVATI and produces two children. He is also depicted as NATARAJA, the Lord of the cosmic Dance. Some

Shaivite texts mention AVATARS (incarnations) of Shiva, but it is the South-Indian devotional tradition, SHAIVA SIDDHANTA, that eventually elevates the god to become the Supreme God of all Creation. (*See also* SHAIVISM)

Shivaratri Festival celebrated in honour of SHIVA held every February/March.

Shraddha / Sraddha An important religious ceremony which is the final rite of passage in Hinduism. Food is offered to the poor and sick and visiting BRAHMINS are given food and coins. The ritual is in memory of departed ancestors and takes place a year after the death of a close relative. It is the duty of the male descendents to maintain the memory of departed ancestors though twice annual shraddhas: one on the anniversary of the death; and the other during the waning moon at the end of the rainy season which is known as the fortnight of the ancestors. (*See also* SAMSKARAS)

Shri / Sri *Lit. illustrious.* Used as a title of respect preceding the name of a deity or holy man/woman. The feminine form is *shrimati*.

Shruti / Sruti / Srti *Lit. that which is heard.* It is applicable to the revealed scriptures, the VEDAS, BRAHMANAS, ARANYAKAS and UPANISHADS, which are believed to have no human authors, but are eternal revelations, breathed out by God at the beginning of each cycle of creation. They are 'heard' by sages in their meditation and passed on orally.

Shvayambhu *See* SVAYAMBHU.

Siddha Legendary holy men with special powers who are believed to live in the high Himalayas as immortals. The term is also used to describe YOGIS who are believed to have achieved exceptional supernatural powers, in particular, those of the NATH tradition founded by GORAKHNATH. (*See also* SIDDHI)

Siddhi Supernatural powers – such as levitation, invisibility, flying, omniscience, appearing simultaneously in different places, withholding breath, curing the sick or raising the dead, or walking on water – that are believed to arise from the practice of YOGA or austerities. Many of Hinduism's holy men and women, particularly those of the BHAKTI or SANT tradition have criticized the motivation of those who practise disciplines to achieve these kind of powers. They argue that the true devotee of God or the adherent trying to achieve liberation should ignore such powers. (*See also* SIDDHA)

Sita   The consort of RAMA and daughter of Raja Janak who was kidnapped by RAVANA, the demon king of Sri Lanka. The RAMAYANA describes Sita's wedding to Rama, her journeys with him in exile, her kidnap by Ravana and her one-pointed chaste devotion to her husband and Lord when in captivity in Sri Lanka. Eventually Rama and the monkeys fight Ravana and destroy him. Sita is released and returns in triumph to AYODHYA with her husband. She is regarded as the exemplar of the perfect wife.

Skanda   The ancient Vedic god of war who is assimilated into the family of SHIVA as one of his two sons. Skanda is also identified with KARTIKEYA, MURUGAN and SUBRAMANIYAM.

Smartas   The followers of SHANKARA who worshipped both VISHNU and SHIVA. They attempted to reconcile sectarian differences through a monistic view of existence. It is also used to describe BRAHMINS who follow a strict orthodox interpretation of SMRITI or scripture. It is often used for Hindus who are prepared to worship both Vishnu and Shiva. (*See also* VAISHNAVISM; SHAIVISM)

Smriti   *Lit. that which is remembered.* The term used for all scripture which is not the Vedic canon, or SHRUTI. *Smriti* refers to tradition and usually implies the PURANAS, including the two great epics, the RAMAYANA and MAHABHARATA. Very often, *smriti* scripture is perceived as the blessings of God upon all human beings as the teachings bring Hinduism to everyone regardless of gender and caste. They are therefore less exclusive than the Vedic texts that are restricted to the top three VARNAS. (*See also* VEDAS)

Soma   The unknown intoxicant used by the BRAHMINS in the ritual sacrifice of the VEDAS. It was believed that the god Indra used the substance and was intoxicated by it. By taking the juice of the Soma plant the participant shared in the experience of the gods. The Soma was drunk as a libation but like AGNI, the god of fire, was believed to be a god in its own right. There was also a Soma ritual where the juice was pressed from the sacred plant and interpreted as the death of the god. Life was given back to the men who participated in the ritual drinking of the juice. The ritual was therefore sacrificial. (*See also* YAJNA)

Sraddha   *See* SHRADDHA.

Sramanas   Non-Brahmin teachers of the Upanishadic period who attracted many followers by their practice of austerity and meditation rather than the performance of ritual sacrifices. (*See also* UPANISHADS)

Sri   The archetypal Goddess and consort of VISHNU who may have been worshipped independently before being absorbed into Vaishnava tradition. In the later mediaeval VAISHNAVISM, Sri is identified with all the consorts of the AVATARS of Vishnu but RAMANUJA taught that she is primeval GURU, the saving grace of God who appears in the form of the guru, endowing that person with compassion and selfless love for humanity. South-Indian Vaishnavism is often known as Sri-Vaishnavism because of the prominent role of the Goddess. (*See also* SHAKTI)

Srimad Bhagavatum   Also known as the *Bhagavata Purana*, it tells of the exploits of KRISHNA, especially the popular mythology of the child Krishna and the time he passed as a cowherd with the GOPIS. The *Srimad Bhagavatum* is an important work for the devotees of Krishna and attempts to reconcile the BHAKTI cult with the high philosophy and ritual of the VEDAS. It is an important scripture for the devotees of ISKCON. (*See also* BHAGAVAD GITA)

Srti / Sruti   *See* SHRUTI.

Subramaniyam   The Aryanised form of the Tamil god, MURUGAN, worshipped in Sri Lanka and Tamil parts of South India. (*See also* ARYAN; SKANDA)

Sudra   The lowest of the four VARNAS. They are not twice-born and therefore have no access to the sacred thread or the Vedic scriptures. They are expected to engage in servile occupations and to serve the three higher VARNAS. It has been theorised that they are the descendents of the people conquered by the ARYANS but, whatever their origins, they have suffered through their low position in Hindu society and are regarded as ritually polluting by the higher castes. (*See also* ARYAN; HARIJAN)

Surdas   (1483–1563) The authentic details of Surdas' life are not known but he was a blind VAISHNAVITE SANT and a prolific writer of devotional poetry in the Hindi language. Six of his poems were included in the final composition of the *Guru Granth Sahib*. (*See also* VAISHNAVISM)

Surya   The god of the sun. Many Hindus offer their prayers to the rising sun at the time of their ritual morning prayers.

Susumna   The psychic channel that is believed to run from the base of the spine to the top of the head, connecting all the CHAKRAS or centres of energy. It is along the *susumna* channel that the KUNDALINI energy travels when raised by YOGA and other spiritual practices. (*See also* TANTRA)

Sutra   A collection of scriptures based on a theme usually attributed to one author and often regarded as the sourcebook for a particular sect or school of philosophy. Usually they are written in a very condensed form as aphorisms. There are many such collections in Hinduism as well as Buddhism.

Suttee   *See* SATI.

Svantantra   A doctrine taught by MADHVA that only God is autonomous. It is only the activity of God that is not dependent on anything else. All other beings are dependent. (*See also* DVAITA)

Svayambhu / Shvayambhu *Lit. self-existent.* This term for the supreme being is used in the UPANISHADS. It is derived from *sva* meaning 'the self' and refers to the belief that only BRAHMAN is self-existent whereas all other beings are dependent. (*See also* ATMAN)

Svetaketu The son of the BRAHMIN in the CHANDOGYA UPANISHAD who is the recipient of the famous teaching that is associated with the unity of ATMAN and BRAHMAN. The son has returned full of pride in his knowledge, but he has never experienced the reality of Brahman. His father teaches him in a series of comparisons that lead to the message of TAT TWAM ASI ('you are that').

Svetasvatara Upanishad One of the principal UPANISHADS, considered as a revelation by the followers of SHIVA as it presents a fully developed treatise on Shiva worship or *bhakti*.

Swami An honorific title applied to a renunciate monk or SANNYASIN. It is derived from *Goswami* (one who has complete control over the senses).

Swaminarayan A large sect of the VAISHNAVITE tradition strong in the state of Gujarat and introduced into Britain and other countries where Gujaratis have migrated. The first custom-designed Hindu temple in Neasden, London was built by the Swaminarayan movement. The movement was founded by Swami Sahajananda (1781–1830) who joined an order of ascetics who were believed to have descended from RAMANUJA. Sahajananda went on to found his own order consisting of around 2,000 ascetics. The movement spread throughout Gujarat. The teachings combine VAISHNAVISM with strict ethical principles and take a reform line on issues such as widow immolation, animal sacrifice and female infanticide. Householders are appointed as administrators of temples and maintain lineages through the male line. Unlike some BHAKTI movements, the *Swaminarayan* movement is traditional in regard to the maintenance of strict caste differentials.

Swaraj *Lit. home rule.* The object of GANDHI's SATYAGRAHA campaign against the British Raj.

Swastika   An ancient Indian symbol of good fortune that is commonly drawn in red dye or made up of flower petals for various rituals or festivities. The four arms signify the four directions (space); the stages in the life-cycle (time) and the four VEDAS (knowledge). It is more significantly used as a symbol in Jainism.

T

Tag   One who renounces the world or practices TYAGA. (*See also* SANNYASIN)

Tagore, Devendranath   (1817–1905) He took over the leadership of the BRAHMO SAMAJ from RAM MOHAN ROY. He changed Roy's emphasis on Upanishadic monism to a more universal form of theism under the influence of the Western-educated middle-class young Hindus who were joining the organization. Under his leadership the Brahmo Samaj took up an active social reform stance to improve the conditions of India's poor.

Taittiriya Upanishad   One of the principal UPANISHADS. The *Upanishad* is cited by Vaishnavites to support the path of devotion to a personal God. It contains references to *bhajananda* (devotional bliss) and *svarupananda* (the bliss of the Lord's form) that can be used to provide ancient doctrinal evidence of the SAGUNA BHAKTI (devotion to form) path. The *Upanishad* also contains examples of ethical behaviour. (*See also* VAISHNAVISM)

Tamas   One of the three GUNAS or qualities that make up PRAKRITI (nature). *Tamas* is usually translated as 'dullness' or 'inertia'. It is often regarded as the lowest of the three *gunas* and its influence in human nature results in sloth and gluttony. Certain foods are described as best avoided because they generate a *tamasic* nature. These are foods which are not fresh or are formed by allowing decaying or fermentation processes to take place. (*See also* RAJAS; SATTVA)

Tandava   One of the dances of NATARAJA, a form of SHIVA. It is a cosmic dance that brings with it world destruction. A legend attributes the first dance of Shiva to have taken place at the famous Shaivite pilgrimage centre in South India at Cidambaram. (*See also* SHAIVISM)

Tantra   A series of scriptures written in the form of a dialogue between SHIVA and his consort, PARVATI, which describe a variety of practices which lead to release through union. Tantra has been developed into a unique path leading to liberation in which the Goddess is the supreme deity. According to Tantra philosophy, Brahman could not create, as it is a neutral absolute, so Shiva and SHAKTI were produced as the two eternal principles of the cosmos. Shakti (the female power) is the active principle that is capable of bringing liberation, whereas Shiva is the cause of bondage. Shakti is the life power of the universe and is identified with *prakriti*. The worship in Tantra paths consists of several overlapping paths. Devotion to Shiva is found amongst many Tantric followers but the unique practices begin with the worship of the Goddess. This is known as the right-handed path (DAKSHINAKARA). Two other paths have generated considerable interest: the first is the left-handed path (*Vamacara*) where the initiate is guided through spiritual disciplines that involve the use of forbidden or taboo substances or practices (MAKARAS) such as drugs, sex and meat. The second is the path of KUNDALINI YOGA where certain meditation techniques are used to activate the Kundalini (serpent power) which is the form of Shakti lying dormant in the human body. The Shakti power rises up through certain centres of energy (CHAKRAS) until it reaches the top of the head. Here it unites with the Shiva power and SAMADHI (union) takes place.

Tapas   Lit. *heat*. The term usually refers to the various forms of austerity practised by ascetics in order to build up their spiritual power. The identification of spiritual power with heat and austerity probably developed by the ancient Vedic correspondence of the heat generated by the sacrificial fire and the heat produced by the efforts of the BRAHMIN performing the sacrifice. *Tapas* was associated therefore with the power of the gods but could be reproduced by the priests either in ritual activity or in devotional fervour. The RISHIS who had received the VEDAS direct from the gods were also believed to possess *tapas* and later Hinduism developed a variety of techniques to develop the power within. Generally, the creation of *tapas* came to be associated with renunciation and austerity. (*See also* AGNI; BRAHMINS; HAVAN)

Tat tvam asi   *Lit. you are that.* This Sanskrit phrase is found in the CHANDOGYA UPANISHAD and various interpretations of its meaning form the foundation of the various types of VEDANTA philosophy. SHANKARA used it to justify his claim that BRAHMAN and ATMAN are identical. MADHVA argued that Shankara had not rendered the meaning correctly and that the true translation was '*That you are not*'. In this way he used it to support his dualistic philosophy or DVAITA Vedanta that argues that the soul and God are distinct and separate. RAMANUJA took up an intermediate position between the two but still essentially saw a distinction between the subject and the object in the phrase, rather than Shankara's more monistic interpretation. (*See also* ADVAITA VEDANTA; VISHISHADVAITA)

Tilak   The caste or sect marks that are placed upon the forehead or other parts of the body using coloured powders or sandalwood paste. These vary from sect to sect and caste to caste. VAISHNAVITES traditionally paint their marks vertically, whereas Shaivites' marks are horizontal. Married women generally place a small dot on their forehead above the nose. *Tilaks* are often placed on the forehead during temple worship. (*See also* SHAIVISM; VAISHNAVISM)

Tirtha   The basic offering of water made to the temple deities and given out to the worshippers who have come to perform PUJA (ritual woship). The water is sometimes taken from a holy river, and can be kept on the family shrine at home. The water of the River Ganges is considered to be especially sacred. Devout Hindus like Ganges water to pass their lips at the moment of death. (*See also* PRASADA)

Tiruvembavai   A famous collection of Tamil hymns to the Goddess which form part of the Tiruvasagam (hymns to SHIVA). The songs are sung during the festival to Minakshi, a South-Indian form of the Goddess.

Tona / Tuna   Magic practices of popular Hinduism used by villagers to cause pain or disaster to those they hold grudges against. It would be necessary to use exorcism carried out by a local expert to remove the spells. (*See also* OJHA)

Totka   Magic rituals carried out by a village priest in order to free a victim of possession by ghosts or the evil eye. (*See also* BHUT; OJHA)

Treta Yuga   The second of the four ages that form the cycle of one round of creation or one day of BRAHMA. Increasing deterioration marks these ages. However, the Treta age is still relatively close to the original golden age and is marked by the prevalence of wisdom in human beings. The human life span decreases by one quarter in each age from an ideal of four hundred years, so in the Treta Yuga, human beings are believed to live for three hundred years. (*See also* YUGAS)

Triguna   The three GUNAS: SATTVA, RAJAS and TAMAS.

Trika   A form of Tantric SHAIVISM once common in Kashmir. It advocated a form of monism similar to the teachings of SHANKARA. Only a few Trika teachers are alive today in Kashmir. (*See also* TANTRA)

Triloka   *Lit. three worlds.* The Vedic division of the cosmos into three worlds: the worlds of the gods, the ancestors and human beings. Each is assigned eleven gods to look over them. All the worlds are part of SAMSARA where the soul can be reborn. Life spans might be vast in the world of the gods, for example, but even gods will eventually die and continue on the cycle of life until final release or liberation. (*See also* BRAHMAN; MUKTI)

Trimarga   The three paths to liberation considered to be the main vehicles for Hindu spiritual practice. They are KARMA YOGA, JNANA YOGA and BHAKTI YOGA. (*See also* MARGA)

Trimurti   The three principle deities, BRAHMA, VISHNU and SHIVA who are said to control the three activities of creation, preservation and destruction which are inherent within the created cosmos. The visual form of the *trimurti* is represented as three heads in one composite deity. Contemporary Hindus, having had contact with Christianity, sometimes refer to this triad god as a trinity but the texts that describe the *trimurti* as three aspects of one God are usually loyal to a particular tradition worshipping only one of the deities. They are, therefore, attempts to indicate that their particular ISHWARA (personal Lord) is superior to and incorporates the other, rather than attempts to create systematic monotheism.

Trividya   *Lit. three knowledges.* The knowledge contained in the three VEDAS.

Tukaram   (1598–1649) One of the four great saints deemed to have died without leaving their physical bodies on earth. The others were KABIR, MIRABHAI and CAITANYA. Tukaram was a seventeenth-century VAISH-NAVITE poet-saint from the state of Maharashtra. The saint did not begin a SAMPRADAYA or movement but today there is a householder group known as the Varkaris who claim to be descendents of his original followers. Images of Tukaram are found in many Hindu temples in Britain, especially those started by East-African migrants of Gujarati origin. (*See also* BHAKTI; SANT; VAISHNAVISM)

Tulasi / Tulsi   A variety of basil tree which is sacred to the devotees of VISHNU or those that follow the VAISHNAVITE tradition of BHAKTI (devotion). The plant is a symbol of Vishnu and the wood is often used to make prayer beads used by Vaishnavas to count the Names of God whilst chanting. (*See also* VAISHNAVISM)

Tulsidas   (1532–1623) The most influential of the mediaeval saints of the North Indian BHAKTI tradition. He was a devotee of RAMA and rewrote the RAMAYANA in Hindi so that the common people would have access to the tale. His version is different to VALMIKI's in that it incorporates the teaching of the *bhakti* tradition. It is known as the RAMACHARITAMANASA and is widely read and loved in North India. Tulsidas taught and wrote in the cities of AYODHYA and VARANASI where there is a temple dedicated to him that has the complete *Ramacharitamanasa* written around its walls.

Turiya   The fourth state of consciousness identified by the UPANISHADS. All conscious living beings are considered to experience the three states of waking consciousness, dreaming and deep sleep. Enlightened humans such as yogis can only experience the fourth state of being. *Turiya* occurs when consciousness becomes completely absorbed in itself rather than the objects of the senses or the movements of the mind. This state is achieved by deep meditation combined with a virtuous life. *Turiya* is indescribable but is experienced as complete freedom, peace and joy arising from awareness of the Self alone. (*See also* MUKTI; SAMADHI; SATCHITANANDA)

Tyaga   Originally associated with the Vedic sacrifice, it referred to the importance of the sacrificer relinquishing attachment to the object sacrificed. As the renunciate ascetic traditions developed in Hinduism, *tyaga* became associated with being detached from the world or living a renunciate's life. However, it is possible to practise *tyaga* as a householder by detaching oneself from the idea of ownership and remaining dispassionate when confronted with worldly success or adversity. (*See also* KARMA YOGA; TAG)

U

Udasis   *Lit. solitary ones.* The first breakaway sect in Sikhism came about as the result of a difference concerning the succession of spiritual authority from Guru Nanak. Sri Chand, the elder son of Guru Nanak, was accepted as GURU by some of his father's followers instead of Guru Angad. They embraced a life of renunciation and therefore became known as Udasis. They continue to be an ascetic order absorbed into the wider framework of the Hindu world but one that gives special reverence to the Adi Granth and Guru Nanak. The rituals of worship conform to usual temple practices of Hinduism such as ARTI. During the eighteenth century, Udasis gained control of Harmandir in Amritsar and many of the historical gurdwaras of Sikhism. This situation continued until the passing of the Gurdwara Act by the British gave control back to the Khalsa. (*See also* ARTI)

Udgatri   A priest who sung the sacred formulas from the Vedas at the fire sacrifice ritual. (*See also* HAVAN; RIG VEDA)

Udgitha   An ancient Vedic term for the sacred MANTRA 'OM' as sung by the UDGATRI BRAHMIN.

Uma   One of the principal names of the Goddess and consort of SHIVA. As Uma she lives in the mountains, especially the Himalayas, where she is the daughter of Himachal, the king of the Himalayas. TULSIDAS recounts the legend of Shiva's awakening from thousands of years of deep meditation in order to meet Uma and marry her. She is considered in his account to be a later reincarnation of PARVATI who seeks to be reunited with her Lord. This story may be an attempt to resolve the various consorts of Shiva into one single entity.

Upadesha   A rite of initiation of a disciple into a religious order or sect under the direction of a GURU. Usually it refers to some kind of religious or spiritual instruction rather than the ritual aspects of initiation. (*See also* SAMPRADAYA)

Upanayana   One of the most important of the Hindu life-cycle rituals (SAMSKARAS) that takes place traditionally during the eighth year of a BRAHMIN boy, the eleventh of a KSHATRIYA and the twelfth of a VAISYA. It is the ceremony that marks the investing of the sacred thread to the members of the three 'twice-born' VARNAS. It marks the beginning of the life-stage when the child becomes responsible for its own actions and can be punished for infringements of DHARMA. Traditionally it marked the beginning of the stage when learning began at the feet of the GURU but today very few Hindu boys will leave home or change schooling. However, it is a still a significant ceremony as it is the first occasion when the Hindu child will take part in religious ceremony in his own right.

Upanishads / Upanisads   *Lit. 'to seat near'.* An important collection of 108 scriptures which reflect on the inner teachings of the VEDAS probably written somewhere between 800 and 400 BCE. The early *Upanishads* are considered to part of the SHRUTI or Vedic canon, and the *Upanishads* are known as VEDANTA or the culmination of the *Vedas* in that they deal with speculative philosophical issues concerning the relationship between ATMAN and BRAHMAN or the way to achieve final release from suffering caused by the chains of bondage to SAMSARA. They are written in the form of a discourse between an enlightened GURU and a disciple often tracing their lineage back to family traditions that were important in the maintenance of Vedic ritual. Although the *Upanishads* could be described as mystical in their content they also contain many references to the Vedic ritual tradition. The main *Upanishads* have been and remain extremely influential and provide the basis of the various forms of Vedanta philosophy. However, they are respected as Vedic literature by most variations of Hinduism. (*See also* BRHADARANAYAKA; CHANDOGYA; KATHA; SVETASVETARA; TAITTIRIYA)

Upavedas Supplementary texts to the VEDAS that deal with non-religious knowledge such as the Arthaveda, the science of statecraft; GANDHARVA VEDA, the science of music and the arts; Dharusveda, the art of archery and warfare; and the AYURVEDA, the science of medicine.

Uttara Mimansa The name given to the various forms of VEDANTA as opposed to the ritualistic PURVA MIMANSA.

V

Vac   The Hindu concept of sacred speech or the correct utterance of the sacred word. The Vedic sacrifice was accompanied by repetition of verses from either the RIG or YAJUR VEDA. Without correct pronunciation and rhythm of the appropriate words, the sacrifice was not correctly performed and invalid. The vibrations of the sacred words connected the human to the divine. The idea of divine speech is picked up again in the BHAKTI or devotional tradition, where the discourses or poetry of a BHAKTA master were considered to be SATSANG (company of truth). The words had a power beyond their message and were capable of connecting the listeners to the experience of the divine.

Vahana   The vehicle or mount of Hindu deities often worshipped as minor gods in their own right. Famous *vahana* are NANDI, the bull of SHIVA; the rat that is ridden by GANESH; and GARUDA, the king of the birds who is ridden by VISHNU.

Vaikuntha   The heavenly realm of VISHNU where he eternally resides seated upon SESA, the endless world snake. According to RAMANUJA and other VAISHNAVITES, liberated souls of devotees live there eternally experiencing the DARSHAN of their Lord. It is, however, common for Hindus to believe that their chosen ISHWARA (personal god) resides in his own heaven where those that are committed to virtue and remembrance of the deity's name will reside. (*See also* VAISHNAVISM)

Vairagya   The quality of dispassion that leads to renunciation. It is the experience of detachment from worldly pleasures that leads to outer renunciation and leads some Hindus to adopt SANNYASIN (renunciate) lifestyles. However, the quality of dispassion is valued highly in Hindu householders as a sign of spiritual progress and leads to inner detachment or renunciation. Some Hindu movements believe that the only true renunciation is inner as opposed to outer.

Vaiseshika   One of the six orthodox schools of philosophy whose origins are attributed to Kanada in the third century BCE. Its two most important texts are the *Vaiseshika Sutras*, possibly written by Kanada himself and the later text, the *Dasapadartha Sastra*, probably written around the sixth century CE. The Vaiseshika and the NYAYA schools are becoming of interest to scholars as they show the formation of early Indian attempts to systematize and develop logic. In this sense, the Vaiseshika is more traditionally a school of philosophy as understood in Western terms than the other DARSHANAS (right views). Salvation is explained as a cognitive process of the recognition of reality rather than intuitive or experiential. Vaiseshika taught that the elements are composed of atoms or infinitely small indivisible parts. Vaiseshika acknowledges the division of the cosmos into the eternal constant and the eternally changeable. The former consists of earth, fire, water, air, ether, time, space and mind and various volitions and qualities. The existence of the ATMAN is inferred from various vital signs such as breathing, love of life and animation.

Vaishnavite   A Hindu who is devoted to VISHNU or one of his AVATARS (incarnations).

Vaishnavism   Vaishnavism, in all its forms, constitutes one of the three major divisions in Hindu worship along with SHAIVISM and Goddess traditions. Vaishnavism is one of the great traditions of Hindu theism and has been popularly promoted through the two epics, the MAHABHARATA and the RAMAYANA, and also through the ecstatic devotional activities of countless saints, particularly of the mediaeval period, who utilized the human forms of Vishnu as their personal focus on the Divine. In this way, Vaishnavite traditions have been influential in promoting Hinduism as a religion that worships one God in many forms. Through the activities of the saints and their followers,

Vaishnavism is divided into countless sects with variations of belief and practice; but the tradition has been given a coherent theology through the work of figures such as RAMANUJA and MADHVA who link Vaishnavism to schools of VEDANTA. (*See also* BHAKTI; KRISHNA; RAMA)

Vaishyas / Vaisyas The third of the four VARNAS; it is traditionally made up of farmers and merchants. They are the last of the three 'twice-born' classes and in Vedic literature are given the duties of protecting cattle, cultivation of land, trade, commerce and performing sacrifice. They are, therefore, the managers and implementers of the economic system and provide the support for the society so that DHARMA can be maintained. In the VEDAS, it is stated that they are born from the thighs of the cosmic person (PURUSHA). (*See also* DVIJA)

Vallabha (1481–1533) A Hindu reformer and VAISHNAVITE who taught the monistic doctrine of identity between ATMAN and BRAHMAN in order to advocate the supremacy of KRISHNA who he perceived as the personification of Brahman. Vallabha advocated householder life as the ideal vehicle for worshipping God and was opposed to renunciation. As with many of mediaeval BHAKTAS, he was opposed to caste or gender restriction in the worship of God. He founded the PUSHTI MARGA which he saw as superior to the other paths to the Divine such as the traditional schools of KARMA, JNANA or BHAKTI. *Pushti* refers to the grace of the Divine that is given to the devotee as a gift but cannot be influenced by any action that the devotee carries out.

Valmiki The author of the original Sanskrit version of the RAMAYANA. According to legend, Valmiki began his life as a brigand but was transformed by a meeting with a forest sage who became his GURU. He performed penance and meditation in order to seek forgiveness for his earlier crimes. Whilst in unbroken meditation, in which ants built their hill over his body, the story of RAMA was revealed to him in Sanskrit poetic form.

Vamacharis The devotees of the so-called left-hand path of TANTRA which prescribes the use of various objects pleasing to the senses that are normally prohibited in Brahmanic or orthodox forms of Hinduism.

Vamana   The fourth AVATAR (manifestation) of VISHNU as a dwarf. The story states that Bali, the ruler of the earth offered a sacrifice in which hundreds of lesser kings and rulers were invited. Each was offered a boon as custom dictated. Vishnu manifested as the dwarf Vamana and asked for enough land to be given to him that he could cover in three steps. The king agreed. The dwarf grew to a huge size and covered the earth in one step; the cosmos with his second and there was nowhere left for his third. The king offered his head for Vamana's third step and acknowledged the supremacy of Vishnu as the Lord of the Universe. One of the principal PURANAS is named the *Vamana Purana*.

Vanaprastha   The third of the four stages of life that comprise VARNASHRAMA DHARMA and should be ideally followed by the twice-born VARNAS. It literally means 'forest-dweller' and indicates a withdrawal from the duties of the world prior to complete renunciation in preparation for death. Ancient Hindu literature mentions that elderly couples would set up a new home on the outskirts of a village and dedicate their activities to the pursuit of MOKSHA (liberation). In modern India, very few follow the custom literally, but many elderly couples try to develop a lifestyle that allows more time for the worship of God once their children have attained adulthood. (*See also* ASHRAMAS; VARNASHRAMDHARMA)

Vanaprasthi   *Lit. a forest-dweller*. The term denotes someone in the third stage of life. (*See also* VANAPRASTHA)

Varaha   The fourth of the AVATARS of VISHNU who manifested as a giant boar to lift the earth from the universal flood waters and thus save her from destruction.

Varanasi   A city on the banks of the GANGA (Ganges) river, also known as Kashi or Benares. It is one of the holiest of pilgrimage sites and an ancient seat of learning. The University is one of the oldest in the world and still trains BRAHMIN priests. The city is sacred to SHIVA and it is believed that he roams the streets at night looking for the souls of those about to die so that he may liberate them. As a consequence, many Hindus come to Varanasi believing that to die in the city ensures liberation. Two of the GHATS that lead down to the river are used for funerals and it is said that the pyres have not ceased to burn for thousands of years. The city's riverfront is one of the most distinctive sights in the world where thousands of pilgrims bathe and perform religious rites in front of ancient palaces and temples.

Varna   *Lit. colour.* The four classes or principal divisions of Hindu society; namely, BRAHMIN, KSHATRIYA, VAISHYA and SUDRA. The first three are denoted 'twice-born' and may take part in the sacred thread ceremony. Many Hindus beleive that the *varnas* were established at the creation of the world and are therefore immutable. This ideal of the *varnas* is supported by the fourfold division of the cosmic man (PURUSHA) described in the RIG VEDA. Others believe that they denote natural divisions of labour according to archetypal human character. This opens up a debate on whether one is a member of a *varna* by birth or quality. Most Hindus retain the idea of membership by birth and do not marry out of *varna*. *Varna* should not be confused with caste or JATI, which refers to numerous sub-divisions within each of the four *varnas*. (*See also* VARNASHRAMDHARMA)

Varnashrama   The four VARNAS and the four stages of life that should ideally be followed throughout the life of a Hindu born into one of the three twice-born VARNAS. (*See also* VARNASHRAMDHARMA)

Varnashramdharma   The ancient Vedic system believed to be divinely ordained, whereby society is divided into four VARNAS (BRAHMIN, KSHATRIYA, VAISYA, SUDRA) and four stages of life or ASHRAMAS (BRAHMACHARYA, GRIHASTHA, VANAPRASTHA and SANNYASIN) where each has specific duties to be performed. (*See also* BRAHMIN; DHARMA)

Varsha Pratipada   *Lit. the day of creation.* Usually celebrated as New Year's Day in Hindu India.

Varuna   An important deity in early ARYAN civilization. He is mentioned in the VEDAS as the god responsible for physical and moral order (RTA). He is also the sky god and the king of the universe. In the RIG VEDA he is next in importance after INDRA and AGNI but he is rarely mentioned in modern Hinduism except in parts of the Vedic sacrifice performed by BRAHMINS at rites of passage. It is argued by some scholars that Varuna was superseded by VISHNU.

Vasudeva   One of the names of VISHNU particularly associated with KRISHNA who is often called *Vasudeva Krishna*. Vasudeva is the one who is filled with all six divine qualities: knowledge, strength, lordship, heroism, power and splendour.

Vayu   The Vedic god of the wind sometimes associated with INDRA. He is also known as the god of the spirit and was born from the breath of the cosmic sacrifice of the primal being according to the RIG VEDA. (*See also* MADHVA)

Veda   *Lit. knowledge.* The earliest body of scriptures written somewhere between 1500 and 800 BCE but passed down as oral tradition. The *Vedas* are believed to have been revealed to fully enlightened sages known as RISHIS and to consist of the following texts, which are all regarded as SHRUTI: RIG VEDA which mostly contains hymns to gods associated with the sacrifice and cosmic order; YAJUR VEDA which contains MANTRAS and ritual formulae for use in the sacrifice; SAMA VEDA which contains chanting instructions for the sacrifice; and the ATHARVA VEDA which contains practices of popular folk Hinduism such as spells and exorcism of spirits. There are three other categories of text that are considered to belong to the Vedic canon: BRAHMANAS which contain commentaries written upon the four Vedas by priests; ARANYAKAS which contain secret or mystical interpretations of the Vedic rituals; and UPANISHADS which contain speculative interpretation concerning the relationship of human beings, the universe and supreme reality.

Vedangas   A branch of explanatory literature used to provide BRAHMIN students with the means to interpret the RIG VEDA and use it correctly in ritual. The Vedangas consist of Siksha, which deals with correct pronunciation; Jyotisa, which teaches astrology and astronomy; Chanda, which focuses on explanation of verse metres; Kalpa, which deals with correct performance of ritual; Vyakarana, the study of grammar; and Nirukta, which provides an etymology of rare words.

Vedanta   *Lit. end of the Vedas.* One of the six schools of orthodox philosophy that is based on the teaching of the UPANISHADS and therefore considered to be the culmination of Vedic teaching. It could be argued that Vedanta is the most influential of the schools of philosophy as it provides intellectual coherence to the teachings of the BHAKTI movement through the ideas of RAMANUJA and MADHVA. SHANKARA's ADVAITA VEDANTA is the exception as it was opposed by the above two VAISHNAVITE figures. The three main proponents disagree over the relationship between BRAHMAN, ATMAN and creation. Their respective schools of Vedanta are called: ADVAITA VEDANTA, VISHISH-TADVAITA VEDANTA, DVAITA VEDANTA. Advaita Vedanta has had a great influence on the intellectual classes of modern Hinduism and even influenced some nineteenth-century Western philosophers.

Vibhuti   Used by PATANJALI to describe the miraculous powers that can be attained from the practice of YOGA, *vibhuti* also refers to the sacred ash from the sacrificial fire that can be placed on the body or imbibed as a magical potion to cure diseases or fulfil boons and prayers. The practice of using *vibhuti* is strong in certain Shaivite traditions where ascetics also daub their full bodies in ash. (*See also* BHABUT; SHAIVISM)

Vidya   Used to describe spiritual knowledge or wisdom. It is used by the proponents of ADVAITA VEDANTA to refer to the experiential knowledge of the unity of Brahman and ATMAN. From the time of the UPANISHADS onwards, a variety of systems differentiate between the eternal reality and the endlessly changing *samsara*. The *Upanishads* and later scriptures posit the existence of both the eternal and the changing existing side by side within the human being who alone has the capacity to disengage from the changing phenomena and identify completely with the changeless and eternal reality. This can be achieved whilst alive. If this process occurs, liberation is certain after death. The process of gaining self-knowledge of one's being as both eternal and changing but increasingly identifying with the eternal is known as *vidya*. (*See also* MOKSHA)

Vijay Dashmi   Another name for the festival of DASSERA. (*See also* NAVARATRI)

Vishishtadvaita Vedanta   The school of VEDANTA founded by RAMANUJA in opposition to SHANKARA's philosophy of unqualified non-dualism. Ramanuja argued that there was a distinct difference between God, the soul and creation. Consequently, the most important relationship is that of worshipped and worshipper.

Vishnu   One of the most important gods in the Hindu pantheon. He is part of the TRIMURTI with BRAHMA and SHIVA as the aspect of the Supreme Being that is concerned with preservation of creation and righteousness. Consequently, it is Vishnu who manifests as the AVATAR in order to preserve SANATAN DHARMA or the eternal religion. Traditionally there are ten *avatars* of Vishnu from the beginning of this cycle of creation. Five are non-human: they are MATSYA, the fish; EKASRINGA, the unicorn; KURMA, the tortoise; VARAHA, the boar; NARASIMHA, the half man-lion. Five are human: they are VAMANA, PARASHURAMA, RAMA, KRISHNA and the future *avatar*, KALKI. However, many Hindus add their own favoured saint to the list of Vishnu *avatars* and millions include Buddha and Jesus. The most popularly worshipped *avatars* of Vishnu are the universal saviour figures: Rama and Krishna. Vishnu is regarded by the countless sects of VAISHNAVITE tradition as the cause of all existence, but he differs from BRAHMAN in that he is a personal saviour God full of grace and compassion to his devotees. The roots of Vishnu worship are found in the earliest scriptures of Hindu tradition and may even be pre-ARYAN.

Vishva Parishad / Vishwa Parisad   The Hindu Worldwide Fellowship founded in Bombay in 1964 as a religious organization with the intention of promoting a unified version of Hinduism that brings all the sects together with an articulate set of beliefs and practices. The movement is often perceived to be the religious arm of the political RSS (Rastriya Svayam-Sevak Singh). Both movements have been criticized for inciting inter-communal violence and are an anti-Muslim and Christian presence in India. The two movements are represented in Indian party politics by the BJP (Bharatiya Janata Party).

Vishvakarma / Vishwakarma   First mentioned in the VEDAS as the Father-God who has made all things, he is now more often associated with particular castes, especially smiths, as the god of architecture who has designed the universe. His image is usually that of a venerable old man with a long white beard whose four arms hold design instruments. In Britain, many Hindu temples contain the image of Vishwakarma; this is probably because many Hindus in that country are from East Africa and were originally recruited from the artisan castes of India in the nineteenth century as indented labour.

Vishvamitra / Vishwamitra   One of the Vedic sages and leader of the Bharata Clan mentioned in the RIG VEDA who probably lived somewhere between 2609–2293 BCE. Tradition states that he was born into a KSHATRIYA (warrior) family but through the performance of austerities received a boon from VISHNU that he could change his caste to BRAHMIN. In the RAMAYANA, written by TULSIDAS, he is the sage who takes RAMA and his brother away from the kingdom of AYODHYA in order to destroy various demons interfering with the religious practices of the forest hermits. (*See also* RAMACHARITAMANASA)

Viveha   The SAMSKARA (life-cycle rite) of marriage. This is an important event in the Hindu life cycle as it marks the passage from BRAHMACHARYA (celibate student) to GRIHASTYA (householder) stages of life. These are part of VARNASHRAMADHARMA which is considered to be the ideal pattern of life for the first three VARNAS (twice-born castes). The wedding ceremony is based on the ancient fire-sacrifice and is performed by BRAHMINS. The bride and groom circumambulate the fire whilst making an offering and their vows to each other. The wife will generally leave her family and move in with her husband's family and be subject to the household leadership of the mother-in-law. Marriages are generally arranged within caste boundaries and are the union of two families. However, traditional ancient Hindu law acknowledged certain kinds of love marriage. Today, the system of traditional arranged marriages within caste is under severe pressure from urbanization and globalization.

Viveka   The important quality of discrimination. Most Indian traditions see the human condition in terms of knowledge/ignorance dichotomies rather than sin/redemption. Thus the ability to differentiate truth from falsehood or reality from illusion, the real from the unreal, is crucial for any progress to be made towards liberation or enlightenment. (*See also* MUKTI; NIRVANA; SAMSARA)

Vivekananda, Swami (1863–86). Famous disciple of RAMAKRISHNA and founder of the RAMAKRISHNA MISSION. Although Ramakrishna was himself opposed to any kind of organizational activity, Vivekananda went on to become the most successful reformer of contemporary Hinduism. In 1893, Vivekananda departed India to attend the World Parliament of Religions in Chicago. He continued to tour America and Europe promoting a Vedantic view of Hinduism that emphasized philosophy and experience of the divine. His championing of Hinduism abroad helped bring a new self-confidence to Hindus and the Ramakrishna Mission helped develop a Hindu social conscience as it organized schools, colleges, hospitals, hostels and relief organizations.

Vratas *Lit. a vow*. An important element of Hindu religious practice. Vows are made to bring blessings for new initiatives or to transform an existing situation by bringing divine assistance. They may also be made by ascetics in order to increase their TAPAS and bring them supernatural powers. Common vows are made to gods by pilgrims in order to secure divine intercession to deal with life problems. Vows often involve fasting or giving up certain foods, practising austerities, renouncing specific sense pleasures for a duration, or going on pilgrimages under specified conditions.

Vrindavan A famous pilgrimage city in North India associated with KRISHNA's childhood and youth. The AVATAR of VISHNU is believed to have passed time in the area of Vrindavan after his exile. It is also believed to be the site of Krishna's various LILAS or divine play with the GOPIS (cowherds). The city is the centre of the Bengali tradition of Krishna devotion which originated with CAITANYA MAHUPRABHU and his followers. It is likely that it was unknown as a site of Krishna worship until discovered by the Bengali mediaeval saint on his travels throughout India. Today it is one of the most important centres of pilgrimage in India. (*See also* GAUDIYA VAISHNAVISM)

Vyasa   A famous sage and devotee of VISHNU who is credited with writing the original text of the MAHABHARATA, including the BHAGAVAD GITA. Tradition states that Vyasa dictated the great epic to the god, Ganesh. Vyasa is also considered to be the author of the MAHAPURANAS. The accreditation of such popular texts to an elevated sage with a status similar to that of the RISHIS who composed the VEDAS may have been a device to gain authenticity for new popular as opposed to Brahmanic texts.

Yadavas   The North-Indian tribe to which KRISHNA was born as a prince mentioned in several scriptures.

Yajamana   The person who commissions a Vedic ritual to be performed and a participant in the ceremony. (*See also* BRAHMIN; YAJNA)

Yajna   Originally used to describe the two kinds of ancient Vedic sacrifice performed by BRAHMINS. The first kind of *yajna* was a public ceremonial event consisting of the sacrifice of a grain, an animal and the SOMA rituals. The second form of *yajna* was performed for a specific purpose on a special occasion in order to achieve a certain end such as extra merit leading to immortality, victory in battle, a birth of a child, good health, long life, prosperity or cure from disease. Offering sacrifices were part of the world order (DHARMA) and maintained cosmic order (RTA). Millions of *yajnas* are still performed especially in the latter category above. Public sacrifices are much more rare. The *yajna*, properly performed, is more powerful than the DEVA (god) who is obliged to obey the power of the sacrifice. Although various *yajnas* may take diverse forms they must have the common elements of sacrificial materials; the mental attitude of non-attachment to the items sacrificed; a god (MURTI) to be addressed as the recipient of the sacrifice; a MANTRA or sacred formula that has power over the god and the Brahmin priests to perform the ceremony. (*See also* HAVAN; HOMA)

Yajnavalkya   A sage who teaches the path to liberation in the BRHADARANYAKA UPANISHAD. Yajnavalkya's teaching represents a major shift away from the ritualism of the VEDAS to an analysis of the physical and psychological states of humankind. In the process, he defines the nature of the self and distinguishes between the lower self, made up of PRAKRITI and the higher Self or ATMAN which he posits is identical to the ultimate and cosmic reality, BRAHMAN. Yajnavalkya purports that it is the knowledge of the higher Self that leads to liberation or the end of the cycle the rebirth. (*See also* UPANISHADS; ADVAITA VEDANTA)

Yajur Veda One of the four VEDAS, it provides the formulas and the precise form of the ceremonies for sacred rituals performed by BRAHMIN priests.

Yama The god of death and final arbiter of rebirth decided by the weight of KARMA or deeds performed whilst alive. Yama appears in several famous stories concerning victory over death. The two most well known are those of SAVITRI and NATCHIKETAS.

Yamuna / Jamuna A sacred river to Hindus and a tributary of the GANGA associated with KRISHNA as it flows through the pilgrimage town of VRINDAVAN. It is also associated with the famous twelve-yearly celebration of the festival of KUMBHA MELA, held at Allahabad where the Yamuna meets the Ganga.

Yantra A symmetrical geometrical diagram such as a MANDALA used in TANTRA as a visual form of meditation or as a symbol in certain rituals. The typical design of a *yantra* is an outer square with gateways containing a design of contentric circles and triangles and an innermost design of arcs forming the petals of a lotus. Everything leads in to the centre of the diagram. Different parts of the *yantra* represent different aspects of the Goddess. The initiate uses the *yantra* to project through the gates and then identify with various aspects of the Goddess until the centre is reached where complete identification can take place. Whereas a MANTRA is spoken, and *tantra* is performed, *yantra* is visualized or seen.

Yasoda The foster mother of KRISHNA during the period that he was exiled from AYODHYA and lived amongst the cowherds of VRINDAVAN. (*See also* GOPIS)

Yatra   Hindu pilgrimage. (*See also* PRAVRAJYA)

Yoga   Yoga is popularized as a system of physical exercises and mental relaxation, but it is mostly varieties of HATHA YOGA that are taught. The term yoga is used in a variety of ways in contemporary Hinduism. It describes methods of self-control and discipline that have a spiritual dimension and also union of the soul and the supreme reality, or a method which promotes that experience; finally it is one of the six orthodox schools of philosophy in Hinduism. The School of Yoga was founded by PATANJALI in the early centuries CE in an attempt to organize a coherent system out of a vast variety of techniques and methods. The philosophy of the Yoga School is based on SAMKHYA but provides a coherent system of practice. Yoga is based on an eightfold path to direct the practitioner from awareness of the external world to a focus on the inner. The first five stages attempt to remove the external causes of mental distraction. The first two stages, *yama* (restraint) and NIYAMA (observance), provide the moral basis for the discipline and help to control unruly emotions. The next three provide the physical environment or discipline for the practitioner. They are ASANA (posture), PRANAYAMA (breath control) and PRATYAHARA (control of the senses). The final three stages are concerned with increasing the ability to control the movement of the mind. *Darana* focuses the mind on one object of meditation; DHYANA is the state where the mind achieves the ability to remain in a focused state of concentration without distraction. The final state of SAMADHI is achieved when subject/object consciousness is lost and there is only the experience of meditation. (*See also* YOGA SUTRAS)

Yoga Sutras   A scripture written by PATANJALI, probably in the early centuries CE, that provided a systematic exposition and elaboration of the path of YOGA as a means of release from the bondage of SAMSARA. The bare essentials of the philosophical school of Yoga are laid out in short but concentrated aphorisms beginning with a definition of yoga as the system of mind-control. Complete cessation of all mental activity is defined as the goal of yoga, in which consciousness rests in itself without any awareness of external or mental distraction. Thus consciousness is liberated from PRAKRITI (primordial matter) and the influence of the GUNAS. The Yoga Sutras describe an eightfold path that enables the yoga practitioner to move from internal to external consciousness. (*See also* SAMKHYA)

Yogananda, Paramhansa   A twentieth-century Hindu SANNYASIN (monk) who travelled to America and Britain and founded the Yoga Fellowship of California. He is more famous for the influence of his book, *Autobiography of a Yogi*. There is no doubt that it helped promote the teachings of Hinduism in the West, especially amongst members of the counterculture in the 1960s.

Yogi   A practitioner of the disciplines of YOGA.

Yoni   A representation of the female sex organ and symbol of SHAKTI (the power of the Goddess) that compliments the LINGAM (a common phallus symbol associated with SHIVA). It is usually formed as a circular construction with a rim that drains away the liquid offerings of milk and water made by worshippers to the *Shiva lingam* that is set in the middle of the *yoni*.

Yudhishthira   The eldest of the PANDAVA brothers, known for his sense of righteousness. He was trapped into a gambling contest with his cousins, the Kauravas, who cheated. As a consequence, the Pandavas lost their kingdom, were forced into exile and began the sequence of events that led to the Battle of KURUKSHETRA as described in the MAHABHARATA. (*See also* ARJUNA; KRISHNA)

Yuga   An age or extended period of time that together form one cycle of creation. After the completion of each age, the creation is dissolved back into primal reality from where it is recreated to begin another cycle of existence. There are four such ages which are differentiated by the degree of spirituality in each one. They are KRTA or *sat yuga* (1,728,000 years), TRETA YUGA (1,296,000), DVAPARA YUGA (864,000) and finally KALI YUGA (age of darkness) which lasts for 432,000 years.

The latter is the current age and will end with the coming of KALKI, the tenth avatar of VISHNU.